THE LAST CHIVAREE

The Last Chivaree

Robert Isbell

The Hicks Family of Beech Mountain

Foreword by Wilma Dykeman

The University of North Carolina Press

Chapel Hill and London

Design by April Leidig-Higgins

Illustrations by John MacDonald

The paper in this book meets the guidelines for permanence
and durability of the Committee on Production Guidelines
for Book Longevity of the Council on Library Resources.

Library of Congress Cataloging-in-Publication Data

Isbell, Robert, 1923– . The last chivaree : the Hicks family
of Beech Mountain / Robert Isbell.

p. cm.   Includes bibliographical references (p.).

ISBN 0-8078-2266-3 (cloth: alk. paper).   1. Hicks family.

2. Beech Mountain (N.C.) – Biography.   3. Hicks, Ray, 1922– .

4. Mountain life – Appalachian Region, Southern.

5. Appalachian Region, Southern – Social life and customs.

6. Folklorists – North Carolina – Beech Mountain – Biography.

I. Title.

F264.B38178   1996   95-42499

974 – dc20   CIP

00 99 98 97 96   5 4 3 2 1

chiv·a·ree (shiv·a·ree) \ shi-vє-'rē \ *n* [from the French *charivari*] (1843): a noisy, boisterous wedding celebration, anticipated by many couples as proof of their belonging in a community, but occasionally having violent or tragic results.

CONTENTS

"Survival skills," "cultural identity and tenacity," "make do or do without": Ways to describe the theme of *The Last Chivaree* are as varied as the readers who will become this book's devotees. But whether the summaries are in academic language or colloquial folk speech, they indicate the value of Robert Isbell's story of one remarkable family of the North Carolina mountains.

A refreshing feature of this book is that first and foremost it is the chronicle of a friendship. We do not meet the Hicks family of Beech Mountain in genealogical order, but in the chronology of their acquaintance with Robert Isbell.

Thirty-three years before his book begins, the author and a young friend snapped a photograph of a clear-eyed young banjo player at a mountain folk festival in Boone, North Carolina. Three decades later that photograph resurfaced and reminded Isbell of the musician "smiling under a cocked denim hat." His story begins with a search for "the Lost Banjoist," whose very name was unknown. That pilgrimage leads deep into the remote mountains (remote from what? the Hickses might ask) and deep into the lives of a family whose roots in this rugged land reach back to the late 1700s.

Stanley Hicks is the subject of that "mellowed picture," and it is his life we enter first. Gradually, naturally, we become acquainted with his wife and his immediate and extended family, and then that of his double first cousin, Ray Hicks, the other major voice emerging from these pages. It is inappropriate to describe Isbell's method as gathering information through interviews or oral history. Those terms evoke a technical approach, an atmosphere of brisk professionalism that is the antithesis of the relationship between this author and his subjects. Here is a bountiful gathering of experiences, of insights and wisdom, growing during long winter days and summer evenings of conversation, walks through fields and woods, and drives along winding mountain roads.

The words, the voices are those of storytellers and ballad makers. Fortunately there are no attempts to render their speech in the phonetic spelling that can create a dialect separating, rather than uniting, speaker and reader. Many past narratives of Appalachian life have diluted or lost the universality of regional experience by a distorted emphasis on uniqueness of language. That uniqueness is valuable, and it is captured by Isbell in his friends' rhythms of speech, certain antique words, fresh turns of phrase or habits of exclamation. But these distinguish each individual's conversation and delight the reader without a burden of apostrophes, misspellings, and wearisome quaintness.

Above all, Isbell is a good listener. He recognizes the understatement that conceals the grief of a tragic loss or reveals the humor implicit in some human predicament. The harshness of life in the mountains is sometimes brutal. Nature is not only the source of beneficent rain and sun, food for nourishment, and herbs for healing; it also can become the sudden destroyer of land and life. Death is part of life, pain is measured out with pleasure, work is the accepted passport to survival. Joy is most often discovered in commonplace events: the routine of days and seasons, courtship, a well-made dulcimer. National honors and the admiration of outsiders are received with thanks and with dignity. But it is the sound of the fox chase, the scampering beagle, the murmur of the creek in summer, and the taste of homemade wine that bring light to the eyes of the Hickses, who have learned to seize pleasure along the middle way between their hardships and their fame. For although both Stanley and Ray Hicks have been nationally acclaimed for their artistry, the recognition changed neither their physical circumstances nor their characters.

In his *Modern Painters*, John Ruskin wrote: "Mountains are to the rest of the body of the earth what violent muscular action is to the body of man. The muscles and tendons of its anatomy are, in the mountain, brought out with force and convulsive energy, full of expression, passion, and strength; the plain and the lower hills are the repose and the effortless motion of the frame." The Hickses of Beech Mountain would have understood Ruskin's words. This narrative, which includes a few of the Hickses' favorite stories and songs, is as deftly woven as any fine piece of homespun fabric. And the pattern that emerges is rich and of much value, the profile of people who lived at one with the mountains' "expression, passion, and strength."

Wilma Dykeman
September 1995

ACKNOWLEDGMENTS

Interviews conducted between 1989 and 1992 with Leonard Ray Hicks, Stanley Hicks, Edd Presnell, and Naomi Shomaker supplied the crux of this story. In addition, Bessie Hicks Proffitt and Frank Proffitt Jr. provided information on Frank and Anne Warner's bond with the Beech Mountain people; these remembrances are supported by Anne Warner's book, *Traditional American Folk Songs* (see Sources). Others, living and dead, who shared essential information include Alfred Adams, Ned Austin, Margaret Shomaker Campbell, Ed Chappell, Bill Cornett, David Hicks, Orville Hicks, Rosa Harmon Hicks, Ted Hicks, Rebecca Farthing Lawrence, Howard "H" Mast, Hattie Hicks Presnell, Nettie Hicks Presnell, Willard Watson, Michael Wagner, and Max Woody.

Since 1950, there have also been those who, consciously or not, guided me into a deeper insight of mountain people and their highlands: Robert E. Agle, Alan Browning, Richard Chase, Sloan Coleman, Charles Elledge, Earl Freeman, Watt Gragg, I. G. Greer, Stanley Harris, Kermit Hunter, Russell D. Hodges Sr., Kai Jurgensen, A. P. Kephart, Harvey Laffoon, George McCoy, Hugh Morton, Claude Ramsey, Grover C. Robbins Sr., Constance Stallings, D. J. Whitener, Mabel Wolfe Wheaton, and Fred Wolfe.

Although in the text I frequently use the present tense to share with readers the intimate and candid quality of the book's subjects, some of these men and women have died since my project began. Also, the names of five characters — none playing a major part and none now living — have been changed as a matter of choice and sensitivity.

I am indebted to Suzanne Comer Bell for her counsel and advocacy, to Pamela Upton for her painstaking and sensitive editing of the final manuscript, to Patricia Estes Coleman for her review of the initial draft, to Peel Calhoun for her search for informative photographs, and to Frances G. Isbell, my wife, for her aid and alliance.

THE LAST CHIVAREE

CHAPTER ONE

The Lost Banjoist

Rains came often that summer of 1955. Mountain husbandmen, driven from their potato and cabbage fields, trekked down from the peaks and coves around Valle Crucis; they gathered on the front porch of Will Mast's old store and told stories of other wet summers. This year was nothing like August 1940, when mudslides had leveled homes and turgid rivers had washed bridges away, yet there was enough rain to keep people from hoeing their crops and grubbing herbs from the soft mountain soil.

Over in Boone, where an outdoor drama about pioneers played, rain too often kept audiences cooped up in their lodgings. Late every afternoon, townspeople gathered on the theater grounds to gauge the coming night's weather. If dark clouds rolled in across distant Grandfather Mountain, sponsors knew the tourists would not venture out; they worried that the drama, in only its fourth season, might not survive beyond that year.

It was folklorist Richard Chase who came up with an answer. Nothing could be done, of course, at those times when rain drifted in, but on nights of good weather, especially the high-attendance weekend nights, it might be possible to lure audiences larger than normal. At such times Chase could bring in storytellers, dancers, fiddlers, and dulcimer players who would welcome the chance to perform before an audience. These were not ordinary entertainers. They came from Watauga County's remote Beech Creek section, a primitive area rarely seen by the outside world. They were descended from Scottish, English, and German settlers who had for two hundred years enfolded themselves in the valleys under Beech Mountain. Lacking good roads, electricity, and many other conveniences of the modern age, these people had remained in an isolation that kept their songs and stories uncorrupted by contemporary life; to most outsiders, they seemed to represent the candle ends of antiquity.

On the first day these performers came to the theater grounds, they stunned and delighted the audience. They stomped through a sword dance, brandishing wooden blades to replicate the weapons first used in this sixteenth-century ritual. They laughed at their own stories, tales handed down from Elizabethan England. They brought their mountain harps, banjos, dulcimers, harmonicas, and fiddles, on which they played "The Pateroller Song," "Drunken Hiccups," and "Pretty Polly." They sang baleful songs, sometimes in strange keys and irregular rhythms. To happier, livelier tunes they tapped heavy-booted feet.

Travelers from Pennsylvania, New York, New England, and the Midwest learned of the festival from innkeepers off the Blue Ridge Parkway. They delighted in the rare candor of the performers. When the players were not entertaining, they would look curiously about the audience. On stage, one fiddler stared at the treetops throughout his performance. A young dancer, her beribboned hat flung from her head in the fury of a dance, ran offstage to chase it.

It was at one of these Saturday afternoon performances that I met a banjo player whose face I never forgot.

I had been taking pictures with an old view camera and had run out of film. I walked up a little hill to drink from a fountain and then rest on a log bench. I could hear the performers and see them through swaying laurel and rhododendron. A girl whose raven hair fell to her waist sang a ballad in minor key. The audience quieted in response to her soft singing.

From behind me, someone spoke. He said it was a pretty song. I nodded and smiled, not bothering to turn toward him. He came nearer:

"Purty girl, purty song."

I turned to see a man, perhaps in his early forties, grinning over his hearty visage. Proud and cleanly scrubbed, he cradled a crude fretless banjo against the bib of new overalls. His cocked denim hat framed a waggish face.

"Did you hear my pickin'?" he asked.

The Lost Banjoist

— 2 —

I admitted that I had not but would like to hear him play the handsome instrument he held.

"Made it myself," he said. He passed the banjo to me, and I rubbed its long neck, feeling precious imperfections. I asked if he would go on stage again.

"Yah," he said. "Gonna play 'Shady Grove.' Maybe ye can hear me then."

He was spellbound by the camera. I took the strap from my neck and placed it over his head. Then I shaded the viewing lens for him to see the image of the girl on stage. He grinned broadly.

"Never had my picture took by myself," he said. "Once there was one with the others at school."

"Never by yourself?"

"Always wanted one, but never had one."

I looked into the face of a man-child; a trust shone there that challenged one to protect him; there was in his blue-gray eyes an expectancy that life would always be good, that brotherhood transcends cultures and boundaries. Indeed, if he said so, a portrait of him had never been made.

"Would you mind if I took your picture?"

"I'd be obliged," he said.

The girl's song ended and the dancers came on. They began to whirl and stomp and skip through a tune called "The Bear Went Over the Mountain." A stagehand came up and told my new friend to get ready to play.

"Well, bye," said the banjoist. "Come down and hear me."

I left the hill and went looking for Paul Smith, an assistant. Paul, a young student, said he would like to take the picture. He had seen the man and had heard him play. Paul went for the film and returned as the banjoist picked his last tune. Then the man stood posing, proudly erect; it was a reenactment of the moment he spoke to me on the hill. His clean-shaven face shone like a schoolboy's; his eyes were clear and alive.

"When the picture is developed," I said, "I will send it to you."

It was a promise I did not keep. Soon after, I moved to Asheville, ninety miles south of Boone, and the picture, now developed, lay buried in my belongings. When it finally showed up in an attic trunk thirty years later, I did not know how to reach the Lost Banjoist. I had always meant to obtain his address from the folklorist who worked with the Beech Creek entertainers, but now I soon learned that Richard Chase was dead. I had failed the Lost Banjoist, and I regretted he would not see the first portrait ever made of him. I wanted to find

The Lost Banjoist

him, to bridge a third of a century, and to learn how life had treated this seemingly happy, guileless human being. If the man still lived, I wanted to close the circle and get to know him. He was remarkable in my memories.

Three years later, I learned of a man living in Watauga County near the Tennessee border who made dulcimers and banjos. I was told he knew most musicians from those parts, and perhaps he could tell me what had happened to my Lost Banjoist. In a rural telephone book I found the name of instrument maker Stanley Hicks. When I called, I told him I wanted him to help me identify a banjoist from an old picture. He said he'd try and that I should "come on up if ye can."

Days later I find Stanley Hicks. His sitting room is uncluttered; framed pictures of dead relatives hang along three walls, and plaques and posters recognize the old man's folk artistry. His soft voice sounds through a quietness unique to old, rarely used country parlors; the images in the photographs seem to speak in whispers.

"Oh yeah, I remember Richard Chase," says Stanley Hicks. "Don't know if I can help you locate your banjo picker, though, but I'll try; I know just about every music maker in these parts."

We talk for a while, and Stanley tells me that health has forced him to give up making dulcimers and banjos. The dust, especially from walnut wood, aggravated his asthma. He says the day he stopped was "about the sorrowfullest time" of his life.

I mention seeing a wall of wormy chestnut the day before, and Stanley says there are still ghosts of chestnut trees in the forests.

"Till the blight hit them, me and my wife would pick chestnuts. We carried them across Long Mountain into Will Mast's store. Will Mast. You know the old store you pass. We'd walk across the mountains and take chestnuts up there and get about four dollars a bushel. Mister Mast would let us swap for stuff that we'd tote home. My wife'd carry the light sacks and I'd carry the heavy sacks."

Stanley says he remembers well when the trees began to wither and fewer chestnuts fell on the forest floor.

"Some people blamed the gooseberry," he says. "They'd get out in the forest and dig up the plants. But that ain't what killed the chestnut trees. You see, the people . . . they got so bad. Little old young'uns pickin' up chestnuts. The people would run 'em out and law 'em. Law 'em because they's pickin' up chestnuts.

"And I think the Good Lord killed the chestnut trees. I think that's what happened. I don't think the blight hit 'em. I think people just got so bad and they'd run the little old young'uns out."

Stanley becomes meditative, and there is an interval of silence. Now seems the right time. From the briefcase I draw out the Lost Banjoist's photograph. For a long moment Stanley inspects the mellowed picture. Then lackluster eyes seem to mist behind steel spectacles. He nods and passes the picture back to me. At last he speaks:

"You're looking at him."

For an instant I cannot reply. I have wished for this very moment for many years, but when it comes I am stunned and disbelieving. Until now I had fancied the man of the picture in fixed time where he did not age. He would always be the happy banjoist of a long-ago day, always smiling under a cocked denim hat. To me his voice should be as strong and clear as it was that summer afternoon of our younger days when he held out his banjo and I rubbed along its carved neck.

The man before me now is gaunt, broken, and colorless. He only faintly resembles the image in the picture; but still there are the large hands, the earnest look, the stately bearing, the clean bib overalls. His speech belies my fantasy; it projects feebly, and at times there is no way to know what he says except by piecing words together in the context of other words.

"That's me," he says. "A real nice picture. I'd love to have one."

Since the negative has long been lost, I will have copies made from the original print; I will give Stanley as many as he wants. Although many pictures have been made of him since that first portrait, this one would be special.

"Just give me one for the wall," he says. "It's a nice picture."

I ask if he still plays the banjo. He tells me he "goes on," but only rarely because of his failing health.

"I go where it's closest around. Don't go much anymore. My asthma, y'know."

We talk the morning long. As one o'clock nears, I suggest driving him over into Tennessee for lunch. I would bring him back and then take my leave. It is an idea he does not like. He asks if I can stay to eat and says he does not want to go out into the weather. He wants to show me his shed, the place where he once

The Lost Banjoist

made banjos and dulcimers. But to stay longer would make me uneasy; I think of his asthma and ask if talking does not irritate his throat.

"You don't know how much this means to me," he says. "It's because I've been by myself so much. You gonna stay, ain't you?"

It has not occurred to me that he shares my enjoyment, and I say, yes, I want to stay. Then he walks me into the linoleum-floored kitchen. Light flows through curtained windows on two sides. He says he will eat cookies and raisin cakes ("I never get hongry; just eat to keep from getting hongry") but that he has meat in the freezer and corn and beans. I choose to eat lightly and take a moon pie and cranberry juice. He suggests that I have wine rather than juice; I beg off "because of digestion," a refusal I am soon to regret. He assures me that the Bible says wine is good for a bad stomach.

"Yeah, it's there. You get the Bible and look it up. . . . It says to drink a little wine for the stomach's sake." He tells of a woman who had visited him. "Criticized me for saying that, but I told her, I said, 'Get your Bible, woman. It's in it.'"

Chastised, I sip the juice and look through the kitchen past the living room windows and on to a range of mountains across the horizon. Stanley says the largest of these is Rich Mountain: "Runs from Mountain City to Boone. And the mountain we're on here is called Stone Mountain. Tennessee's on the other side of it. And Beech Mountain is to your south. You can go up yonder, go here in my field and take the glasses and watch them ski. Now if you want some corn flakes, I'll get you a bowl . . ."

"Oh, no thanks," I interrupt. "This moon pie is quite enough."

He says he is sorry I do not take the wine, that he is concerned for my stomach.

"They's a preacher come here and his wife and another feller and another lady. They mentioned wine somehow. And I said, 'I got some good wine.' Well, one of the women, she raised Cain. I said to her, 'No,' I said, 'You go to the doctor?' She said she did, that she went every year for a checkup. And I said, 'You take his medicine?' She said she did. And I said, 'You ever look on it? See how much alkyhol's in it? Some of it's thirty percent.' She said, 'Yeah, but the doctor 'scribed it.' 'Well,' I said, 'I'll 'scribe you the wine.'

"Well, the four of them got some, and we set around here, and they got ready to go, and the preacher said, 'If you don't care, I'd like to have a little more of that wine. For the stomach's sake.'"

The Lost Banjoist

Stanley wryly pauses, and the quietness of the house and the outdoors settles about us. Slowly he chews on a raisin cake, while his sunken eyes scan the field toward Stone Mountain's peak. I study him now, still trying to equate this aging man and his many infirmities with the ebullient banjoist of thirty-three years ago. His dark hair is only sparsely touched with gray, and the mustache has been grown since I first saw him. Today, with Pointer overalls, he wears an open-collared flannel shirt of red and blue plaid, and he is cleanly shaven. As he renews his lecture on wine, dark brows arch and his eyes shine with a hint of his younger days.

"I told the preacher to do everything in moderation. You can eat too much, drink too much, work too hard—it ain't the wine. I told the preacher to go in there and get more wine 'cause he said it was about as good as he ever drank. I make wine every year that comes. I make some wine.

" 'I'll tell you another thing,' I told them. 'Used to be, they had sacraments in the old Primitive Baptist.' And I said, 'They used wine in it, and a little hard bread.' And I said, 'Noah got drunk on wine, and the young'uns laughed at his nakedness.' And I said, 'They's punished fer it.' Then I said, 'You must not read your Bible.' The woman never said any more."

Though the sun is shining hard, there is a mountain chill. With both hands, Stanley fits a felt cap onto his head. He pulls from the closet a mackinaw faced with cotton twill and lined with sheepskin, its wool exposed at wide, pointed lapels. Now he will take me to the shed where he made the banjos and dulcimers. It is a visit I do not ask for, because I am still concerned for his asthma, but it is clear that Stanley wants to show off his workplace, a cherished corner of his past.

"Can't work there any more 'cause of my asthma. Wood dust from the dulcimers, especially walnut dust."

We walk slowly to the shop in the side yard. Above and beyond, Stone Mountain hovers over the gray-brown March countryside, and the sky is cold and without clouds.

The three-level shop is built of blocks. On the entry side, an evergreen vine climbs from ground to roof. The whole structure seems ancient, remindful of a peasant cottage in the Old Country. The lean-to entry is accessed by seven steps that climb to a tin-roofed porch. Grotesque gnarls of bleached wood crowd along the length of a crude wooden rail. These serve partly as a barrier against falling, partly as a repository for whimsical potpourri.

The Lost Banjoist

We climb the steps and I stop to inspect a large piece of driftwood. Stanley comes over: "Now my son's cow. She got her foot hung down in that hole; carried that root in the field all day. I went down there and got it off and got David to go down and bring it up here." Stanley has often picked up driftwood on his farm. "Now that's a one-headed giant." He indicates a piece with a swirled knot. "We used to tell these tales, and they's a one-headed giant and a two-headed giant and a three-headed giant, and one with four heads. The old king was trying to get these giants killed. See, they was taking his grass. And that's a one-headed giant right there. Look at his nose. See his nose? See his eyes?"

Stanley is meditative now. He lives in several planes: the hard life of his reality, the nether world of his own phantasmagoric making, the past from which he selects memories, and the world of the Bible according to his own interpretation. Now his attention moves to a device that, he explains, is a turkey trap.

"When I don't want to kill a turkey, I take it out and let it go, but most of it I give away. There's a trigger here [he laughs at some secret memory] and it goes down through here. The turkey goes back here and tries to get out." He cackles, and I realize that Stanley is suddenly younger. He is in his favorite world and is laughing for the first time.

"I caught a polecat once. Caught two beagles."

He talks about his grandfather, about how the old man trapped the wild turkeys: "Dug a trench and built a pen out of poles. Put grain on the trail. The turkeys would go into the ditch and they'd fly up into the pen; didn't know how to get out."

When Stanley was a small boy, he asked for a large turkey his grandfather once caught. "I wanted that big old gobbler . . . beard that long [he measures with his hands] but Grandpa said the turkey would fly away with me. Which I guess he would."

Inside, the shop is cold. Pictures, plaques, a mirror, ox horns, and a deer head adorn the paneled walls. The patterned linoleum floor is well swept, and the workplace is as clean as his home. A dozen or more alarm clocks rest on the crude workbench; in front of them lies a dulcimer.

"The last delcimore Dad built."

He tunes the instrument and then begins to play a lively piece he says is called "Skip to My Lou."

If I shut my eyes I can hear ancient bagpipes, their notes skirling along the long halls of an old Scottish castle. When the playing finishes, I tell Stanley his music takes me back in time. He seems embarrassed and moves along the bench.

"Ha," he cries. "And right there's the first banjo I built, when I's fifteen years old. And here's one Dad built long ago."

Fervor builds. Out of context, he says I must go see his cousin Ray. "He's got a stove you want to see. Fixed it so it throws off more heat, he claims." Stanley is smiling again; it is obvious that he is proud of Ray. Now he turns back to the dulcimer. "My dad built that in 1931. Right here's my mother's picture before she was married . . . and one beside it is Grandpaw . . . never did meet him . . . horse kicked him to death. And over here's one of my mother and her daddy, a preacher, Andrew Pressley, the grandpaw the horse kicked."

Back in his house, Stanley picks up the picture I brought. He chuckles and says he was prettier thirty-three years ago. Now he goes into an adjoining room and brings out a banjo—not the one of the picture, he says, but the last he used in "concerts."

"No, can't go to concerts much anymore, 'count of my health. I'm laid up now; health's got bad . . . [ravens caw outside and Stanley's words are not clear], but the only rich person in this world is a well person. If your health's good, it don't difference. See, when your health gets bad, why you can't enjoy anything."

When spring comes, Stanley will move the double bed from the sitting area back into the room from which he fetched the banjo. In the big room there are two stoves—one for wood, one for oil. On frigid nights, when the northwest wind cries, two roaring heaters barely keep him warm. His bed is placed between both fires so that he might survive the winter.

Now he takes up the banjo and sits forward in the vinyl-covered lounge chair next to the bed. He tunes the instrument and breaks into a song called "Cripple Creek." When he finishes, he explains that he used to play clawhammer-style, but he cut off the tip of a finger making dulcimers, and now that finger is too short to strum clawhammer anymore.

"Here's 'Chicken in the Corn on Sourwood Mountain.' Don't pick much no more on account of m'health." He plays again, calling over the music: "That banjo has been around a lot."

With a flourish, he ends the tune but remains sitting forward in the lounge chair. He looks past the window and far beyond Old Pete Field to the Rich

The Lost Banjoist

Mountain range. Old Pete Field? "Yeah," he answers. "Old Pete is the man who once 'stayed there.'" Stanley now drifts into silence, and I think that perhaps his voice is weakened by the asthma. I ease up from my chair to leave, but suddenly he speaks again:

"Two years ago, three winters ago, I fed the birds up there in that hole. Fed 'em scratch grain. So I made me up a song." He takes up the banjo and begins to strum and sing.

Bird's in the bush and bear's in the den
The fox in the hole and snorin' again
The river froze over and the creeks went dry
Got no wings and I can't fly
I went home and got in the bed
I pulled the cover down over my head
Pulled the cover down over my hea-a-d
Pulled the cover down over my head.

Got up next morning and the moon went down
Sun come out jest layin' on the ground
I got up and went back to bed
I pulled the cover down over my head
Pulled the cover down over my head
Pulled the cover down over my hea-a-d
Pulled the cover down over my head.

Got up that night and made a little round
I met Miss Sadie and I blowed her down
Met a good run, would have been slow
Sharp overhaul named Jerico
Took me downtown, dressed me in black
Put me in a freight train and sent me back
Put me in a freight train and sent me ba-a-ack
Put me in a freight train and sent me back.

Bird's in the bush and bear's in the den
The fox in the hole is snorin' again
The river froze over and the creeks went dry
Got no wings and I can't fly

The Lost Banjoist

I went home and got in the bed
Pulled the cover down over my head
Pulled the cover down over my hea-a-d
Pulled the cover down over my head.

Laying down the banjo, he gets up and walks to the window. Ravens cry
again, and the sun is tepid upon the sill. Stanley says he has always liked the
house, but it "wasn't built right." He tells me he lost a barn in a storm two
months ago.

"Yeah, bad storm come out of the southwest. Never have seen it do that before. Never have. I've been in the mountains all my life. Never saw nothing like
it. Just sat here and dozed all night in the chair. I mean it broke treetops out, it
blowed trees across power lines, ripped off tin roofs. Been some time in January. Boy, it was rough. Lord ha' mercy.

"It come thisaway, come out of the west. Never in my life. And I had my dog
tied down there. My daughter-in-law across the road went down and crawled
under the trees and turned the dog loose; he hadn't been hurted. Crushed his
bed though. Ha! Bet he thought thunder 'n lightning hit him. Crazy thing. No,
hit blowed and took the whole first shed—forty-five long and twenty-four wide.
And it rambled all around . . . sounded like a cyclone or something. Left everything a-sitting where it's at. Never blowed a thing out of the shed. Just took the
top and the metal roof and all that, the sides and all. Left the things inside and
didn't hurt my dog."

Outside a beagle puppy sees Stanley through the window and wags his tail
and shimmies his whole body. Stanley stares and grins.

Ever since the National Endowment of the Arts named him a National Heritage Fellow, Stanley has entertained strange people from places he never heard
of. "Come by the busloads sometimes," he says. "Bless their hearts. Want to
give me money." They ask him to play the banjo, to sing outrageous songs; they
want to visit the shed where he made dulcimers. Unfailingly, Stanley obliges—
an old mountain man who would rather talk about his dogs and whose memories are rooted in Old Pete Field and in the days when he played and stomped
about on a crude stage to the lusty merriment of his audiences.

Through the window he looks out across a rinsed sky. His gaze seems not focused on the scene but instead is one of remembering. Tourists are good company, but they are no substitutes for foot-tapping, roisterous, Saturday-night

The Lost Banjoist

hootenanny audiences. Nor does Stanley want to tell his curious visitors about how he listens to his dogs in the chase.

He shakes his head: "They don't understand."

The room smells faintly of linoleum and oak. Stanley looks toward Old Pete Field and sees a small animal run toward the house then swiftly change course and scamper into the woods. The beagle, occupied with Stanley and still shaking about, does not see the animal.

"Might be a rabbit," says Stanley. "Now, that beagle pup out there. He don't want to go with the old dog. Wants to go by hisself. Wants to be on his own.

"I went down the road and set there in a warm place, and that pup rambled on in front till he was out of sight. Directly I heard him barkin'; never heard such barkin' in my life. I said to myself that there ain't no rabbit down there, and I soon found I was right. It was a polecat. I said, 'My God. I don't want that polecat stuff on him. But I finally got the pup and put a leash on him. That beagle'd run anything that makes a track—any kind of rabbit, groundhog, possum . . . he'd run another dog's track."

From his lounge chair Stanley reaches and pulls the banjo snug to his body. He sits forward and his pale eyes look far away into the light and he makes no sound. Then he cradles the banjo and slowly plucks the strings as he talks.

"This one I made up—a fox chase. Had me three foxhounds once. Old Bush, Old Cripple, and Old Blue. Now Old Blue was a good dog. I'd rather hear him run foxes than any dog I ever saw.

"Here, now listen. They're pretty shiftless when they want to be, but I'm gonna see if I can get them going." He shouts, "Blue . . . Cripple . . . Bush!" By following Stanley's eyes, you know the dogs are jumping and yelping and ready to go.

"Whoo," he says, and he begins to play. The first notes sound slowly, as though the dogs are puzzled and sniffing. Then a loping rhythm indicates they are moving out.

"That's old Bush." The pace livens. "Here's Cripple . . . hah!" Still faster the strumming goes.

"Now, Old Blue! But they ain't got it going real good yet. They just on the trail. Whoo! Hah!"

The sitting room that seemed stale and cavernous begins to echo to the banjo and to Stanley's whooping.

"Whoo! Hah! Gettin' hot." Now the banjo's rhythm slows and the tune undulates, seeming at times to skip beats. Then the throbbing returns as if the dogs were picking up a stronger scent. The volume reaches a new level. "Old Blue! Now they've got it going. Old Blue jumped! Whoo! Hah!"

Stanley turns his head in such a way that you know he is hearing the dogs; the banjo is imitating the dash of hounds through the brush, trees, fields, mountains.

"They's coming back off Stone Mountain and I'm a-feared they'll run through my tobacco patch. If they do, you know what'll happen? They'll tear it all to . . .

"Hah! Whoo!"

The banjo's pace is fevered now. The old man's eyes are ablaze.

"That Blue can go! And the fox—his ol' tongue's a-hanging out. Hah! They draggin' it out, but Old Blue's up near the hole. I can tell. Whoo! Hah!"

Suddenly there is silence and a pause. Out of the quiet, four high notes are plucked and the chase seems finished.

"Went in the hole right there," says Stanley, pointing to his feet where lino-leum covers a trapdoor.

"Whoo! Hah!"

Now he relaxes the banjo. It is time for me to applaud because I know that in his reverie a stomping, whistling, and clapping audience responds lustily.

A sadness hangs about his person; it is the longing of an old warrior who bat-tled unconquerable enemies but made life bearable by private enchantments. He gleaned meager crops, gathered herbs, built houses and barns, walked thousands of miles, and saw his family through harsh winters. And, in his days of glory, he stood with a homemade banjo and saluted rollicking Saturday-night audiences. He would not trade these experiences for those of an ancient king.

Stanley was appointed. He carried messages, both happy and forlorn, that came to him from his parents, his grandparents, and their grandparents, reach-ing back even to the first forebear to "enter" this mountain land. The ballads he played came from the England and Scotland of long ago, and the songs sur-vived the intervening years and were still flavored with Elizabethan overtones. He played the banjos and dulcimers he made in his shed, and he smiled as he reflected upon his uncommon craftsmanship.

Now he is in the last years of his seventies. He has asthma and a strange feel-ing in his abdomen. All the loves are gone from his house: an adoring wife who bolstered him when times were tough; a grown son who now lives across the

The Lost Banjoist

road and must arise before dawn to work on the highways; the fox chases; and finally the buck dancing, banjo picking, dulcimer playing, and ballad singing that drew yells and whistles from hardy crowds in meetinghouses throughout the high mountains.

His wife's long illness drained what was left of the old man's wiry strength. When finally she was taken to the "nurses home," he missed having her in the house. To comfort her and lengthen her life, he traded nearly all his possessions. Now, on this windswept day, he wonders if he was born too late, if perhaps he was "not fittin'" for the twentieth century.

"Used to be that old folks was left to stay in their homes. It weren't no problem; nobody went to a nurses home because they wasn't none. People didn't go to orphanages, either, because somebody would always take in a young'un to have an extra hand on the farm. But the way people's a-living now is different. We didn't have money back then, but we was fixed to take care of sick people. We didn't try to squeeze a few days more out of their lives . . . make them unhappy because they're not at home. And having tubes running out of them so you can't hardly tell who they are when you go see them. No, they was still the kings and queens of their homes. And their homes, no matter what kind of shack they lived in, was their palace. They might have died six months sooner but they got to stay home where people loved them."

Stanley says he learned hard lessons from seeing people like his wife, Virgie, spend their last days among strangers:

"When I start to go—and that might not be far off—I want my son to know that I don't care about all that fuss. That ain't helping much anyway. I want to die at home if they'll let me. That way I won't be taking away so much money that others need to live on. And I'd druther be here to look out of the window when my dogs start barkin'."

Outside, the little beagle is looking up. Stanley lays the banjo down and walks closer to the window. As though the beagle has understood when his master mentioned dogs, he rears up and paws the air. In a charged moment of time, a grinning old man and a frisky young dog share happy, secret adventures. Spring will come, and soon there will be foxes and rabbits waiting in the meadows and woods beyond Old Pete Field.

"If you ain't got something to pass off the time," says Stanley, "you just up agin it."

The Lost Banjoist

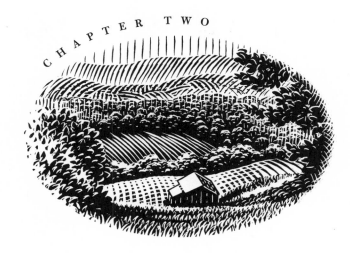

CHAPTER TWO

A Tough Life... but a Gift of God

Want and need were constant attendants to Stanley Hicks and to all his kin, past and present. It matters not that his ancestor David Hix (later Hicks) owned hundreds of rich valley acres in the 1700s, or that Stanley himself was invited to Washington to accept an award as a national treasure. Hardship clouded the existence of Stanley and everyone he knew.

"See, they wuddn't no jobs, wuddn't nothing to do," he says. "We raised what we eat, eat what we raised. And what money we had would go to pay tax . . . maybe a pair of shoes a year."

What wonder then that—though bereft of regular schooling, muscled out of the mainstream, relegated to a place of insignificance—the cast and ilk of Stanley Hicks carry an indefinable dignity. They speak an unruled and uninhibited language, and when they tell of the past, they transport listeners along a corridor of mystery.

On Hattie Hill, Stanley Hicks enjoys the status of nobility. He claims his own worth and is granted his independence. He has no inherited wealth or power or land, but his heritage is one of hardened dignity that sets him apart. Though he is growing old and lives on the edge of poverty, he enjoys a freedom that few others dare attempt. To him, outside culture has no value because he adheres to the tenet that surplus does not create happiness. Despite a legacy of want, Stanley has been master of his expectations. Only now, with his health failing, does he face losing the accouterments that have given him happiness: the frisky, frolicking puppy, the dulcimer shed, the crafted banjo, and the expanse of Old Pete Field.

In the still, lonely night when he cannot breathe "on accounta my asthma," or when his cancerous stomach throbs, he lies awake or gets up and sits in his lounge chair; at those times he thinks of the dogs, the dulcimer making, the buck dancing and banjo playing, the rough cheering of the crowds. He glories in the memory of his mother and father, who also played fiddles, guitars, banjos, and dulcimers. Now Stanley himself is not far from his eightieth year. He has worked hard and received little money for his labors, but he wonders if the young people of today are "coming up right" and if they are really happy without knowing want: "All of them asking for cars, so many on dope, so few that take care of theirselves."

A neighbor who lives a half-mile down Hattie Hill says he never knew anyone to say anything bad about Stanley, that Stanley "makes everybody feel good." Other neighbors and hill people have their own stories of the man's generous ways.

Once when Stanley had gone down to Asheville for a concert, he saw a black-haired girl whom he thought lovely in every way. Someone told him the young woman wanted to meet him. It was then that he discovered she could not see.

The girl told Stanley she had waited for him all day, and Stanley said, "I'm here. What'll you need?" The girl then asked if he thought she could ever learn to play a dulcimer. He told her a blind person would find it hard, but that if she worked at it, yes, she could. He laid his dulcimer across her lap. She ran her fingers across the strings, and there were incidental notes, sweet and random tones she had never heard so near to her. Presently she stopped and rubbed the walnut body of the instrument. Tears welled in her eyes, and Stanley told her she had a nice touch, that if she loved the instrument she could learn to play it.

She asked how much a dulcimer would cost. Stanley gave her a price but said he was busy, that maybe sometime later he'd have time to work on one.

Back on Hattie Hill he told his wife that he intended to make a dulcimer to give to the girl, but Virgie protested. She reasoned that Stanley labored hard to bring cash into the house, and his giving away a week's work would be generous beyond their means.

A Tough Life

"But," said Stanley, "it's the right thing to do."

The next day at the shop he selected prime black walnut wood, even though he knew the girl could never see it. When he finished, having put this work ahead of paying jobs, he packed the dulcimer carefully for mailing. He put a note inside that said the only charge would be that the girl send a picture of herself with the dulcimer.

A letter soon came back. Inside was a snapshot of the girl strumming the instrument. She wrote that, by its feel, she knew it was a fine work; she would learn to play it.

In the time he could manage away from farm chores, Stanley crafted more than five hundred instruments. In the early days, he sold dulcimers for ten dollars but, before walnut dust stopped him, that going price grew by fifteen times. Yet Stanley still gave away banjos and dulcimers to people dear to him. In the end, whatever money he had put into his life savings went to the "nurses home" to pay for his wife's care until she died.

Stanley Hicks has known life to be onerous, but he does not admit to poverty. He endures hardships as an expected part of his existence; his lot is made bearable because adversity has been constant everywhere around him—among the people he loves, his kin, his neighbors, his forebears. The ways of humanity are not meant to be easy. Stanley accepts his destitution as honest and right. When a neighbor needs him, he gives, as he once gave his banjos and dulcimers.

He is curiously proud of his hard life: he steeled his gaunt body against want; he toughened his will by pitting his mind and energy against adversity. He has helped forge an austere culture that still endures, and his penury has separated him from outside civilization more certainly than geography.

"It's been a tough life, but it's a gift of God," he said. "Atter I was married I'd take my stuff and walk all the way from Spice Creek over the mountain to Butler, Tennessee. In winter, rain would freeze and I'd come home with my clothes iced stiff. But I enjoyed life; it was tough and it made *me* tough.

"See, we lived off the farm. We had hogs, we had chickens, we had cows, and we had a few sheep. Everywhere we went we had to walk. It was ten miles to Butler, and I walked twenty miles a day, ten there and ten back."

When Stanley, Virgie, and baby David outgrew their first home—an abandoned sawmill—they were given a small parcel of land by Stanley's father, Roby. On this plot they built their first cabin.

"I bought an old crib from a neighbor. It was of kiver boards. We built a house, but it didn't have a ceiling in it, just the roof over our heads that my dad and me kivered. We took an old froe, that somebody later stole, and we rived a fork of a tree and made shingles. We kivered the house with that, but there would be cracks.

"When winter came it would blow snow though the boards on the roof, and with no ceiling to stop the snow it'd just come on down. Me'n my wife would just kiver our heads with a quilt, and when morning came we'd shovel snow back and sweep it out of the house."

From a steel barrel Stanley made a stove. He hammered lengths of metal roofing around a poplar sapling pole and fashioned a smokepipe.

"People today don't know nothing about it. They look at me when I tell them some of these stories about Hoover's Panic and they say, 'That man's crazy.' But I've been out in the zero days of winter with nothing on but a pair of overalls and a union suit. Cold. Wind a-blowing. Don't see how I did it, but I was strong and had a young woman to take care of."

When Franklin D. Roosevelt became president, Stanley Hicks got a job with the WPA and again walked to Butler. He left at four o'clock in the morning, worked all day with pick and shovel, and arrived home at nine in the evening. He earned a dollar a day.

When the WPA projects at Butler came to an end, Stanley joined migrant laborers working on farms in New York State. He first planted his crop at home, then climbed on a freight train and rode the rails with the hoboes. He worked most of the summer in New York before coming home to help his wife harvest their crop.

The Hickses moved from place to place. They rented, bought, built, and rebuilt cabins. The first acreage they purchased had an old house on it. They bought a calf and raised it. Meanwhile Stanley worked for another farmer for seventy-five cents a day.

"We just kept a-going until finally we paid for the little farm."

Son David played about the farm and grew up happily dealing with a scant childhood. He inherited his parents' grace and patience. He worked hard and dedicated himself to his family. As a grown-up, strong and hand-callused, he revered his parents and has never moved far from their home. Given the choice of living today or in his parents' time, he would prefer the way they came up.

"I'm not sure we're not living against ourselves in these times," he says.

Stanley's oldest living sister is nearing ninety. For most of her years she has lived hard, but her wrinkles seem etched from smiling. The summer is young, but she sits before an unlighted oil stove because that is her chosen spot, no matter the season. Regal and neatly coifed, she grins and at times laughs weakly as she speaks. Her face is gaunt and chalky but not so wrinkled as her thin arms. With a small and shaky voice she presides. Her young kin sit about the room and stand in the doorway; they strain to hear her and speak only when asked; they respect her knowledge of days before they lived; they venerate the struggles of her early life.

Hattie Hicks Presnell has triumphed where others faltered; she has survived gracefully through a steel-hard existence that left her crippled. She no longer washes clothes in the creek; she no longer cooks and cleans. But all this she did in her younger days, first for her parents and siblings, then for her mate and her children.

She has lived for many years in this house, to which she and her late husband added rooms as the need arose. The rambling, wood-frame dwelling is comfortable. Its sitting room has a picture window, and through this undraped glass Hattie looks out upon the forests where she and her mate scoured the rich earth for herbs and plants, afterward bartering their harvests for white flour over at Will Mast's store. In the quiet of night, Hattie hears the murmur of rock-littered Beech Creek just outside her bedroom. She lives in a setting that a person of wealth and leisure might envy.

Hattie's great-great-grandfather "entered" not far from here in the last days of the 1700s. He paid but a few cents an acre for both hillside and valley; but by the time Hattie came along, ownership of much of the land had long before left the family.

Her peach-colored, crisp frock conceals the signs of a rugged life. It is not easy to believe that this dainty woman grubbed the soil and once suffered a mangled arm in her father's gristmill.

"When people's arms and legs got crushed, there was no way to get them to a hospital," she recalls. "When this arm got tore up in the mill, I managed to stop the grinder and just grabbed a tow sack and wrapped it around my arm to stop the blood. Never did have a doctor."

Hattie's is but one of many stories of backwoods people tending their own injuries. As she says, people did "what we had to do" in times of tragedy. If a leg was mutilated and developed blood poisoning or gangrene, a friend or family member dosed the victim with strong whiskey and severed the limb with a handsaw.

"Now this other arm. Hurt it bad once and went around here with people saying I ought to walk all the way to Banner Elk to see a doctor. But in a while it came around. I just didn't use it much. Then finally one of my kinfolks got me to go to a doctor. The arm had been broken in four places."

She displays both forearms. Except for sagging flesh and age spots, the limbs show almost no signs of long-past trauma. Hattie smiles to show these trophies of the old days, hard times she endured and conquered.

She knows by family lore and by a wrinkled and faded copy of a will that her great-great-grandfather came to this country well before the Revolutionary War, but except for his name she does not know, nor does she have an interest in, the country he came from or why he chose to settle in these mountains.

"Just wanted to get away, maybe," she says.

Several months after last seeing Stanley Hicks, I return to the Watauga area. In my briefcase I carry photographs of the Lost Banjoist. I intend to take a picture to Stanley and help him hang it next to his trophies and posters.

I stop at the office of a friend and ask to use the phone. I say I want to call Stanley Hicks. My friend asks me to wait; he goes back to his office and returns with a weekly newspaper he has folded to show a story at the bottom of the front page.

"Meant to send this to you last week," he says.

I know before looking: Stanley Hicks is dead.

Across Hattie Hill Road, past a weathered barn and down a long pathway, David Hicks is repainting the tin roof of his modest house. To him, the only son of Stanley, I bring copies of my photograph of the Lost Banjoist. David invites me to walk over to his father's house.

"Just about like it was when you were last here," he tells me as we cross the road. "I'd really like to keep it as he left it."

The house is neat and in order, just as it was when Stanley tended it. The grass is trimmed and the sitting room looks the same as the first time I came there. Pictures, posters, and plaques hang in their old places, but David points to two spots where frames are missing.

"I offered each of my grandchildren something to remember their great-granddad by. They took various things, but one of them wanted the certificate Dad got from President Reagan; the other wanted Dad's picture with his banjo. Except for those, the things you see here are the same Dad had on the wall."

My gaze goes directly to two photographs that had fascinated me during my earlier visit: the only two ever made of Stanley before I met him. In one, his mother holds him in a family portrait; in the other, Stanley stands barefooted with others from his primer classroom. As Stanley told me, there had been no picture taken of him alone until that day of the folk festival.

Memories unfold as David speaks of the strength and gentleness of his parents.

"You talk about tough: Dad did things we can't believe today," he says. "I remember he had a toothache—always had troubles with his teeth—and it was killing him. He took a screwdriver and turned a screw up into his hurting tooth; then he tied a string to that screw; he fixed the other end of the string to Mom's old smoothing iron, walked out on the porch, and threw that iron into the yard. Jerked that tooth out.

"And one time he was plowing over there at Grandpaw's old place. You know, they'd try to plant stuff around stones—more nutrition they said—and the plow turned the dirt right up under the boulder. You know how soft the dirt is here in the mountains. Well, just as Dad passed the rock, plowing behind the horses, that rock tumbled. It knocked Dad down and pinned his leg. He yelled for help all afternoon, but nobody could hear him. He strained and tried his best to move that rock, but it wouldn't budge.

"Then Dad called on them horses. He knew it'd mangle his leg, but he said he'd just take his chances rather than lie there and die in the field. He held on to the plow handle and let the horses yank him out from under the rock. Tore his leg all to pieces; he had trouble with it all his life. But he didn't believe in doctors; he was like an Indian."

David remembers his black-haired mother, Virgie, as a "tender and tough"

A Tough Life

woman who always talked softly. For ten years she worked in Banner Elk and did not miss a day, even though she once fell in Beech Creek and broke an arm; later she fell on ice near her house and broke the other.

The patience with which Stanley and Virgie approached life is reflected in David. Oddly, he sees his own lot today as luxurious. But when snow and ice cover the roads, he is out long before daylight, the day's first traveler over the twisting road down Stone Mountain to Bethel Road. When there is snow, he drives a plow to clear the roads before people start to work. On such days he never sees daylight from his own home.

David thinks he is lucky to have a job working on the roads, but he thinks the challenging life of his parents would have been more to his liking.

"You take today. You make a lot of money. Have a job. But it takes a lot to live. When I was a boy we had no light bill, no phone bill. We didn't want those things because our neighbors didn't have them; nor did they have a fancy car or a big television set. Back in my parents' time, everybody was in the same boat. But times have got better; people better educated, and they've got better-paying jobs. But are they happier? I don't know.

"Back when I was coming up, we got out and cut our wood, raised what we ate, lived free. We'd eat hog meat and had no problem with cholesterol. We'd work it off—didn't know there was such a thing. And the people lived long lives."

David's body is hulking and formidable. His face is bronzed from sun and wind. He dwells often upon the illustrious Stanley, but he says he has neither his father's talent nor his whitleather strength:

"You'd look at Dad and think he wasn't strong; but I'm here to tell you he had power. People today spend a lot of time lifting weights or jogging, but the old people were strong without doing things like that. They'd lift weights all right—bags of fertilizer, beans, taters, and stuff like that. All day long. They'd have slapped their thighs laughing if they'd seen somebody gruntin' with barbells."

David laughs softly. He is thinking of his father and how those days were the "real times," while today young people are "just playing" at life. Also, he is surprised that so many memories are beginning to surface. When he began talking he said he could not recall much of the old days. Now the recollections roll. His eyes crinkle and he smiles often when he talks of his father.

"He must have logged every mountain between here and Morganton. He'd leave over there at Beech Creek, him and Wesley Pressley. They'd be gone all week and come in on weekends; then they'd leave again on Sunday.

"They'd go logging with the old crosscut saws. Used to cut timber down there at Tellwind and South Mountain. Dad said that when one of those big trees came down and hit the ground, rattlesnakes started singing all around him."

Although he regrets the loss of primeval forests, David knows well that timber-cutting jobs were a godsend. Long before he was born, lumber companies had built roads and railway lines into the virgin mountains. The products they took from the forests built many houses, but the axes and crosscut saws left gashes and gaps in the great hills. Topsoil that had accumulated over eons eroded, clogging the pure streams; nutrients washed to the sea and aquifers dried up. The mountains were never the same once loggers ravaged them; but the cash earned from working in lumber camps kept many people of the hills from want and starvation.

David thinks the pace of deterioration has not slowed; it has just taken a different form. Outside his home on the slopes of Stone Mountain, he looks over the terrain.

"When I was a boy none of this timber was cut. There were no fields down below this meadow; it was all woods. I helped cut that timber out there. Helped saw it. We cut hemlocks out there and, Lord have mercy, when we got it to the sawmill we'd have to cut it like they say, buckwheat it. We'd cut a little bit off and then turn the log over. Logs were so big that the saw wouldn't reach through them; just hit the edges. Some were so big that we'd have to take a tractor to lift them onto the skid; we couldn't turn them with hooks, they were so big. We cut timber in here for about two years."

He openly wishes that there were some way to reap the richness of Stone Mountain and still preserve its beauty.

"I used to go up to New York and work on farms, and I'd come back in the fall and think: There's no place like this place, no place.

"I get out here and sit on the hill and just look the country over. The summer is green and smells good; the fall is clear. I wish it could be like this forever, but I know it can't."

He sweeps his arms toward the rolling land beneath Stone Mountain. Scattered about are homes that were built since David was a boy.

"As the world keeps growing and all, it's going to get less beautiful everywhere; there's going to be more houses built on these hills. It will finally take the beauty of these hills away.

"I know people have got to have somewhere to live. Now you can set up a factory and make about anything you want. But land you can't make."

The old ways imprinted David Hicks's childhood. He has precious memories of woodstoves, sleds, horses, oxen, and hoedowns. He remembers the first cars to come into the area and how, in the midst of modern advances, the slower, more primitive ways still prevailed.

"I did homework by an oil lamp. Still have that old lamp somewhere here in Dad's old place. I remember counting out galax leaves and tying them in bunches of twenty-five for Mom and Dad to sell. You see, Mom and Dad would go out and pull galax on the mountain. Work there all day. Then they'd come in with these big hemp sacks loaded with galax. We'd sit there and sort out the leaves under the lamp. We'd count leaves and fix bunches while Dad told Jack Tales as he worked."

David watched his father devise and innovate, saw him carve out a better life by thinking out new ways of doing things.

"I didn't have toys except those he made me. When I was little he made me a rifle from a piece of pipe. I started out to church and Mom made me stuff the rifle into a hollow tree. When we got back to the tree, I reached in and pulled it out and there was a big black snake wrapped around it.

"Dad made all kinds of toys. One was what they called a dumbbell. Dad would tie a hide over a hollow log and fix a knotted string to it. He'd pull that string and it'd make a noise like a bull hollering."

But the "toy" David enjoyed most was the one his father made by taking a seat from a junk Model-A Ford and nailing it to a sled.

"We'd go places in that," David says, "and the thing I recollect most about that sled was one time when we went down to Grandmaw's. She gave me the first loaf of bread I ever saw, and I was tickled to death; held it all the while I was there. Then we started home in the sled and along the way Paul Pressley and a bunch of them came by on horses. Well, Dad got to laughing and racing them in that old sled. Our horse tossed its head high and kicked up its heels and made that sled run. It kicked gravel all into my bread and I was squeezing my loaf so hard that when we got home, the bread was a pitiful thing to see. But I ate it, and it tasted wonderful."

David closes the door and locks Stanley's house. David's own son has urged him to make the place into a museum and let people come to see the dulcimers and banjos and mementos of the life Stanley lived as an instrument maker and musician. David is not sure he wants to do that; he thinks perhaps the place should be kept as it is so the memories will stay private and fresh.

Before his death, Stanley Hicks balked when doctors told him his stomach should be taken out. He asked David to take him home. David prepared a cot in the front room of his Stone Mountain dwelling, and there his father waited to die. In his last hours Stanley could hear the barking of his small dog as it chased rabbits across Old Pete Field.

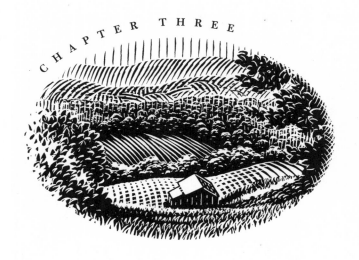

CHAPTER THREE

The Valley of the River

Spring comes slowly to the mountains. Beneath late winter skies the earth snugs under a pale blanket, and cold weather can linger into June.

On such a chilled morning in March 1989, I am traveling toward the sparse vicinage of Ray Hicks, whose "double first cousin" Stanley Hicks said I should visit. The distance to Ray's house from my starting point at Valle Crucis is farther than I have reckoned, but the drive over the bleak countryside blunts the rush of time. It does not matter that by my own schedule I am tardy. Ray Hicks has no telephone, does not expect me, does not know me. Yet I want to be out early, for there is much to do. It seems reasonable to expect that Ray will be awake and stirring when I arrive.

Stanley has told me sketchily how to reach his kinsman's house. Soon I discover that his directions are for those who live in the backcountry, not for those who normally drive city streets. I continue to look for Stanley's landmarks—the narrow wooden bridge, the steepled chapel, the rushing branch, and finally the blue mailbox that tells me I have arrived at Ray Hicks's place.

The morning darkens, and the gray, still landscape takes me back to the novels of Thomas Hardy. No creature stirs in the fields or around the houses and barns, nor does smoke rise from chimneys. I make false passes down roads that all look much like the ones Stanley described. At last a mail carrier approaches. I bring the car to a stop; with no other signal I have let the man know I need attention. He pulls alongside me and turns down his radio.

"You look like somebody gettin' ready to be lost."

"Already lost," I reply, laughing. "Trying to reach the house of Ray Hicks, the storyteller."

"Well, you just missed the turnoff," says the grinning postman. "Turn around and follow me; I'll point to the road when we get there."

In moments we come to a nearly hidden intersection; the man jabs his finger in that direction, then waves happily as he drives away on the higher road.

Dry sedge and leafless trees—dark wraiths of winter—preside along the crude road. Downhill to the right, the dead land flattens into a broad valley. Beyond, a long blue line of high mountains shimmer cold and remote.

I stop at the blue mailbox. Down a steep hill, wood smoke rises from the chimney of a hulking, weathered house. The scene is not unlike Stanley Hicks's description from the day before: A large, unpainted dwelling, down from the road, off to itself, with land falling away to the distant mountains.

For long moments I leave the engine running and look down upon the scene. Firewood stacked high on the porch and a well-worn path to the springhouse speak of hard work and few social frills. Color and prettiness may come from yard flowers in summer, but today the old place is lifeless and melancholy. Yet I find an untold beauty in the surroundings—the long view of the valley and mountains, the strangeness of it all.

On the porch ceiling are hex signs, and the door at which I knock is time-worn. Though the house, as I am to learn, is less than a hundred years old, it has the scent and feel of antiquity.

Minutes later a small and trim woman, perhaps in her late fifties, opens the door. She wears a simple print frock, and her head is framed by tightly swept black hair; she has the look of a Grant Wood farm woman. Bright, dark eyes fix upon me, direct and searching. She does not ask my name. My visit is not expected and she does not know me; yet she pulls the door wide.

I introduce myself, but she does not invite me to sit. She says that Ray will be out "directly." I put down the notebook and camera bag and look about the room as the woman disappears into the kitchen. She does not call to her husband, but there are stirrings from the room to the side. He has heard and knows there is a visitor. Then the woman reenters; she carries a straight chair and hur-

The Valley of the River

ries to set it down by the upholstered chair along the front wall. Without speaking, the woman has led me to understand that her husband will sit in the stuffed chair, close by the warm, antediluvian stove.

She throws a large split log into the heater and settles herself into a caned oak chair. She sits as at attention, and we talk of the weather, of the difficulty of getting good directions. She laughs.

Another door now opens. Ray Hicks, in overalls, hair mussed from sleep, shuffles into the room, his long frame bent but towering. He seems unaccustomed to small courtesies but takes my offered hand. His wife, having seen my camera and having already exacted my business, tells her husband: "I think he's working on a story." Ray crosses the dim room and seats himself slowly in the big chair.

"Yiah, Rosa," he says, brightening, "I figgered he looked like somebody 'ud be writing something."

He waits now for me to confirm their guess. I tell him that I have been with his cousin, Stanley, and that there seems enough material for a book. I say it might be that I knew Ray at a folk festival in Boone thirty-three years ago, and that I met his cousin Stanley at that time. I was with an outdoor drama, and my bride taught sixth grade the winter before at Cove Creek School.

He says nothing, but with one great hand pours tobacco from a tin onto a swatch of cigarette paper, which he holds with the other hand. Then, astonishingly, with the fingers of only one hand he rolls the paper into a crude fag. After wetting the paper along the seam, he puts the soggy tube into his mouth and lights it with fire from the stove. As he stretches his six-foot-seven body, his legs poke out so that his feet rest near the heater. He seems to meditate, his hands fiddling with tobacco paraphernalia. Then he talks into the dimness and silence of the old house. His speech has an uncommon resonance; it seems to come from another time.

"It was at the elemental school where you say y'r wife teached that a woman named Jennie Love first got me to telling stories, 'bout thirty year ago.

"Jack Tales. Jennie Love. She was the daughter of Jack Love that lived across, back down the river from Cove Creek, over on the other side, what they called Rush Branch, where she was raised.

"And her dad, now, was Jack Love that rode the horse with the medicine on it, you know, the medicine he carried on the saddle, that rode through the country to bairn . . . be with the mothers when the babies were bairn, and be with them when they had fever and cold.

"And his daughter Jennie, she was never married.

"That was back when no money much was in the mountains, and she had sent me a cyard, a postal cyard. She knew I'd been a-telling stories ever since I was little. I'd started telling ghost stories learnt from my grandfather and the others. And she sent a cyard. Would I come? Tell stories to her class.

"I was young and everything, and I was running a '39 old car that I'd got off'n anothern for forty-five dollars . . . 'cause he couldn't find what was wrong with the motor. It was a pretty good car and I got it straightened out. I was a mechanic, you see, trained on my own. And I fixed the car, found what was wrong with it. A lot of things wrong with it, the motor . . . a witchy thing . . . a-a-a-h . . . that no mechanic couldn't fix at the garage.

"And so I took that car. Didn't have money to get gas with, and I was running credit of the old Mast's Store, if you know where it's at, at Valle Crucis, with Mister Howard Mast. His daddy built the old store 'way back . . . his father, Will Mast. Now, I don't go in debt for gas or nothing much—it's so hard to pay a debt in legal—so I try to make my way and not go in debt for much except fertilizer and seed to farm a little here. Irish potatoes, I raise them in this rough grade.

"I went to Mast's Store: 'I want a dollar's worth of gas, and you set it down on my ticket.' And so Mister Howard Mast came out and run me in a dollar's worth.

"And I went on over there to the schoolhouse. Never been in there, you know, and I went in and spoke to the principal: 'Jennie Love sent atter me.' Kept the cyard, a-holding it in my hand. 'And now will you'uns take me to her room? To where she's at?' They took me to her room.

"'I don't remember you that much,' I said to her. 'But this is Ray, Nathan Hicks's boy, that knows your dad, and you've been to my home.' I said, 'Your dad's been there, the doctor, back when I can just barely remember the first time. And now I'm here and you want me to tell stories.' She told me she did. And so when I got done, about an hour, she says, 'I'm going to give you three dollars out of my own purse for gas.' And the second trip, she called me again, and again gave me three dollars out of her own purse.

"Then she called me back again and I told tales. Got done, and when I got up to leave, here come some other kids, pretty good-size boys. They said they was a-going to start a war here; said it wasn't fair to get Mister Hicks to tell stories just in her room."

He pauses and, with eyes wide and hands high, whispers: "Ga-a-h. They gonna start a wa-a-r."

He is quiet again, and he snuffs out the cigarette.

"They heard a little bit of it, you know, maybe a-peeping around through the door, and the teacher's trying to keep them quiet, probably. 'Well,' Jennie Love said, 'Mister Hicks, can you stand it with your voice, to go through the rooms?' I said I'd try, and then I went through all the rooms.

"That's how I got started telling the Jack Tales some thirty years ago, there at Cove Creek. Because of Jennie Love. Lived in the valley of the river."

Ray is thoughtful as he draws upon another cigarette. He says most stories are old, but they contain truths.

"I make up some of the stories. And it's me in some of them—things I've done and seen . . . like when Jack and his mother were seeing it hard. See, Jack and his mother was starving in the story called 'Grinding at the Mill.' That's the gristmill I used to go to."

After his appearances at Cove Creek School, Ray's renown as a storyteller grew. In the early 1970s he "started" the storytelling festival held in Tennessee's oldest town, Jonesborough, and said he soon became the "lead man" at a festival on Beech Mountain. His name had become known to ballad and story collectors. Among the numerous television crews that visited his home were crews from London who taped a show for the British Broadcasting Corporation. An American writer saw the documentary and wrote a profile for the *New Yorker*.

"They come here and tell me: 'I know why so many people come atter you. Ain't anybody like you left.'"

In 1983 Ray was asked to come to Washington, where the National Endowment for the Arts named him a National Heritage Fellow. The same award went to his cousin Stanley because he still made dulcimers and banjos in the way of his father and his forebears. The cousins and Rosa were driven by automobile on the long trip across Virginia. They stayed in Washington for a week. Ray told Jack Tales, and Stanley made banjos from groundhog hides and wood he had brought from his Hattie Hill home.

Restaurant food was not as tasty as their beloved home meals, and the mountain men were not at ease in a modern hotel. A week was enough for them, though never before had they seen so much money ($5,000) as they were awarded.

Stanley became sick and each morning had to coax his aging body to meet the schedules. Ray and Rosa were always concerned; having Stanley there was like bringing a bit of Beech Mountain with them.

"It was different," says a laughing Ray. "We got lost in the hotel. Me'n Stanley got caught in a revolving door and it took me two days to get out; we ain't heard from Stanley yet."

The irony in their lives is that both Ray and Stanley were bathed in recognition—by scholars, film makers, television hosts, civic groups, writers, program makers—but, except for the award in Washington and one trip to Atlanta, little money came to them.

After they began to appear in the news media, people would come to their doors, as I had, to see firsthand these living relics, the last of a species all but gone from the earth. Reporters and photographers found their way to both houses; they would direct the Hickses to hoe corn, chop wood, pick herbs, tell stories, and play and sing. A "thank you" was the only reward.

Later Ray had to turn down a few profitable offers "because of my gout atheritis." He could not accept an invitation to appear on the Johnny Carson show. And when a farming group out West wrote and offered a tempting stipend, Ray could not accept that, either. The *Today Show* once sent a crew "to camera me" when Ray spun stories at the renowned Jonesborough festival. Other than for this annual trip into Tennessee, he received only small honoraria from civic, church, and library groups. But visitors to his home on Old Mountain Road often left modest tips.

Ray continued to tell stories to all who came to his home, but Stanley began to withdraw from public attention as his enfeebled body failed him.

On the acreage around his old home, Ray Hicks had plowed the same fields and cleared the same earth his father and grandfather labored upon. In the time of their might, all of them raised crops—mostly potatoes, tobacco, and cabbage. Here, too, father Nathan Hicks made "mountain tea," a distillation of teaberry plants that chewing gum makers used for flavoring.

In 1914 Ray's brawny father raised the house of rough timber cut from his own land. His grandfather, the tall and handsome Benjamin Hicks, who lived down the hollow, came to help. Even great-grandfather Samuel came with his ancient broadaxe; he hewed the joists and sills that helped form the house's foundation. Before winter came, the small group finished the carpentry, laid the stone for a fireplace, and covered the roof with shingles cut from wild chestnut logs.

Eight years later, on August 28, 1922, Ray was born in the front downstairs bedroom, just off the sitting room. Except for two short absences, both spent within the vicinity, he has remained in the same house all his life. It is today the oldest dwelling left on Beech Mountain, its tin roof rusting and its sides painted only with the patina of time. An L-shaped porch skirts the front and right side, and much of the year firewood is stacked to the height of the hex signs. The house is airy and primitive, but Ray measures all he thinks and says from its focus.

He and Rosa reared all their children in the house's drafty rooms. Now their living offspring are gone—all but brawny, dark-bearded, and diffident Ted, who tends the farm and takes care of his parents with quiet strength.

In the years when the Hicks children ran through the lupine and foxglove herb plots, and when they played about the springhouse and the great ash tree, Ray's own youth lengthened; he saw himself in other days playing upon the same spot of earth.

Ray doggedly nursed and groomed this "rough grade" and subsisted from its harvests. With a double-edged axe, he cut firewood in its forests. Even should his fortunes turn into the fabled gold of his Jack Tales, he saw no reason to leave this home; he would live here until they carried him in a wooden box to the crude graveyard of his forebears, who lie buried less than a hundred rods away, beside a nearly impassable, stony road.

Ray warms up to his guest. He rolls another cigarette and again stretches his long frame so that his body forms a triangle with the chair's seat and back. Obviously at ease, he talks of oxen, banjo making, the "bairning" of babies, and of cats whose masters have died. Suddenly he asks, "You want to hear a Jack Tale?" Lost immediately in thought, he does not wait for an answer.

"I been telling these stories since my Grandpa Benjamin passed them on to me when I was a little boy shelling thrash beans on his porch. They ain't really to believe because a lot in them ain't true; but when you're listening, you got to believe."

Thinking of a story to tell, Ray slowly and deeply draws on his cigarette. Finally, he says the story is called "The Three Sillies," and it tells of Jack and his wife, who were "seeing it hard." He pauses again and puffs on his cigarette, gathering his thoughts. Then he drops the cigarette to the old oak floor and snuffs it out with his foot.

"Ah now," he says, "in a lot of these stories, Jack gets married. People say he musta married a lot of women. And so this'n starts off after Jack marries a fine woman."

Her mama gave her a milk cow to help her get started—just like my mama did. And that's all they had, was a milk cow, one that would give them some milk and butter.

Well, they got started and after a while they were up agin it bad. So Jack's wife told him to go out and sell the cow. "When we get to doing better atterwards we can get us another cow," she said.

So Jack asked his wife, "How much you want to sell the cow at?" And she says, "Sell it for fifty guineas."

So Jack took off with the cow, with a rope tied to a halter on her. Directly the cow went through a bee nest, and, gosh, that makes a cow really carry on, them bees a-stinging her and Jack trying to hold her with the rope. And she run around Jack and the rope wrapped around his legs and throwed him down and drugged him around and skinned him up considerable.

About that time, when he was all tangled up there, up come a farmer driving a hog, with a halter on the hog. The farmer said, "Man, whoever you air, look like that cow's a-giving you a lot of trouble. So let me swap my hog for your cow." Jack says, "Believe I will." So they swapped and Jack started on a-driving the hog. Gosh, they's stout, a hog is, like a cow. And maybe a few bees got on the hog, too, 'cause it got excited and was going whuh, whuh, whuh, and it wound around Jack. Gah, it's rooting and dragging him.

And while he was trying to get untangled, up come a man a-carrying a house cat in his arms. And he said, "Stranger, whoever you air, that hog's really giving you a rough round." Jack said, "Bedad, yeah." And the man said, "Let me swap ye this cat for the hog." Said, "He can catch mice and be good around the house." Jack said, "Gah, I just bedad, I believe I will." So he got the cat, carrying it in his arms, and the other man went on with the hog.

Well, Jack got to a creek a-running there with a little old road, and the cat seed a bird, and tried to jump out of Jack's arms so it could catch the bird. Well, it was a-squirming and yowling, and it turned and clawed Jack right down the face, and the blood a-running and all.

Right then come another man who had nothing. But when he seed what a rough time Jack was a-having with the cat, he picked up a round rock where creek water had smoothed it down. He said, "Here, stranger, whoever you air, let me swap you this beautiful rock for that cat." Said, "Gah, it's giving you a-clawing, the way your face looks." Said, "This rock will make a good door prop." And Jack says, "I believe I will." So he just turned around and, a-holding the rock, he started back home.

When he got there, his wife says, "Did you sell the cow?" And Jack had the rock a-holding it under his arm, agin his body. "No," he says, "I didn't sell her, but I swapped her for a hog." His wife says, "Oh, well, we could have some hog meat to eat." Said, "That'll be good as a sold cow, probably."

Jack says, "Well, I met a man with a cat. Swapped the hog for a cat." And his wife said, "Well, that's pretty good." Said, "We've got a awful lot of mice and rats around here."

"Well," Jack says, "the cat tried to spring on a bird, with me a-holding it. It just went k-e-e-ch, and clawed me here, you see, down my face."

Said, "Then a man come along and asked me to swap the cat for a rock. He said it'd make a good door prop."

And Jack's wife then took the rock out of his hand and said, "Door prop!" Said, "My good cow gone, and what I've got now is a door prop!" Said, "How we gonna live, Jack?" She pointed a finger at him and said, "I'm a-leaving you and not a-coming back until I find three fools sillier than you air." And Jack says, says it low, "I bet you can't, honey."

So she went on with her apron on, and she come to a gristmill pond. It was a-getting late and the moon was a-shining down in the water. And they's a man there a-hollering, "Oh, ho, gah." Said, "The moon's fell down in the pond and now I won't know when to plant my corn and stuff, the seasons, you know." And Jack's wife walked up and said, "I can tell you where the moon is at." The man says, "Woman, if you'll tell me where the moon's at, I'll give you ten guineas." She said, "Up yander's the moon, and the shadow's in the water." And she got the ten guineas and put it in her apron pocket.

The Valley of the River

She went on and directly heared a racket. It was a whipping with a whip and a man a-hollering, "Oh, oh, oh." She got on there and then saw a woman in the field who had her husband hooked up to a plow, plowing the gyarden, a-beating him with a whip. And Jack's wife looked up across the fence and said, "Is that you'un's ox up there in the field?" He says, "Yeah, honey, who-ever you air." Says, "We've got the ox but we don't know how to put the harness on it." Said, "If you could show my wife how to put the harness on that ox and hook it up to the plow and get me out of this, I'll give you fifteen guineas. Cash." Jack's wife went up and got the ox, let the bars down and come down and put the harness on the ox, and hooked it to the plow. Showed them how to plow, and the man paid her the fifteen guineas. She put it with the other ten guineas, and that made twenty-five guineas.

She got on to the next house and heared a racket on the porch: Ka-pow, ka-pow. And a man on the porch would go, "Oh, lordy, honey." And so Jack's wife went on up and spoke to them. Turns out that the wife made her husband a shirt every twelve months but she didn't know how to cut a neck hole or sew no button holes, or nothing. And the wife had to put the cloth over her hus-band's head and beat the cloth with a stick of stove wood so that his head would come through. And the wife said, "Gah, if you could show me how to fix a shirt," said, "Gah, it nearly kills him every time we put a new shirt on him." Said, "It beats his brains out to cut a hole through the cloth; cutting it through with a stick of wood, beating his head through the cloth and him a-hollering." And the man says, "Woman, if you can learn my wife how to fix a shirt without me getting punished like this — it nearly kills me every year — I'll give you twenty-five guineas." So Jack's wife took a needle and scissors and made him a real nice-looking shirt. Fixed the neck hole and the collar on it, and put in button holes and fixed the thread around them, and sewed on the buttons. He said, "Here's twenty-five guineas and I don't regret giving it to you, woman, whoever you air."

Jack's wife went on walking and got kinda wore down. Got hot. She come to a log beside a little old path. She set down on it to rest. She was exhausted with the heat. And atter she set there and got cooled some, she got the guineas out and looking at them. Counted them: Ten guineas from the mill pond, and fifteen guineas where the woman was a-whopping her husband with a whip. Said, "Ten and fifteen guineas makes twenty-five." Said, "And there at the house where the wife was beating the shirt over the man's head and nearly killed him, they gave me twenty-five guineas." Said, "Oh, that's fifty guineas. That's what I wanted for my cow."

And said, "Jack told me I couldn't find three people as silly as he is." Said, "I'm going back to stay with him." And she went back with the fifty guineas out of her cow.

Her and Jack lived together till he deceased.

Pleased that he has cast a spell, Ray searches for some sign that reaffirms his artistry. I put down my pen and tell him that the story is fascinating.

"I have it on paper," I say, "but there is no person who can tell such a story the way you do." I want to say more — that I never knew anyone who might convey a simple fantasy with so much beauty. Written words could never grasp the fidelity of Ray Hicks's narrative, told in his own theater.

Rosa says nothing. She has listened to Jack's adventures through untold tellings. Still in her caned chair, she sits absorbed. She has been known to tell Ray he is getting carried away, that he should not talk so much, but today she seems pleased. She is smiling.

Neither Rosa, nor the children, nor any kin know why Ray speaks so strangely. Some say he is the last mountain man to speak Elizabethan English; but this is likely an uninformed notion. Rather, Ray might have harbored the rhetoric of grandparents and great-grandparents well past the time that other mountain people abandoned it. Elizabethan speech folded into an evolving language long ago, a language that changed gradually no matter how isolated the speakers. But in the coves and hollows of Watauga, the old settlers retained many expressions of Anglo-Saxon pioneers.

Ray Hicks uses antiquated words that might come from times even before Shakespeare. He says "skiffin" — found in *Webster's* but rarely heard today — meaning a membrane that often covers a newborn's eyes. He says "bairn" for born, "steer" for oxen, "legal" for currency; his speech is sprinkled with expressions such as "odd gosh," "dodie wood," "granny woman," and other words that might have come from medieval England and Scotland or perhaps from early American usage.

Or again, these ways of speaking that Ray has retained might have been brought into use no farther back than the days of great-grandfather Samuel or even grandfather Benjamin; the vivid expressions are examples of rural talk that has been shamed into oblivion by schoolmarms and later by the ubiquity of television. But Ray is little affected by standardized speech. He reads but sparingly, and outside influences reach him only through festivals and the constant visits of the curious. He does not own a radio or a television set.

Ray loves company, and when guests come he quickly positions himself at the head of the pecking order. He is anxious to talk and can hardly bear his own silence. He knows that he is not always understood. Nevertheless, the more company he entertains, the more quickly his language fades into the commonplace.

Nearly twenty months after that first visit, I come to Ray Hicks's home again. His speech is still lyrical and he repeats phrases for emphasis; but there are changes. When I first met him, he said "bairn" for born. Now he interrupts himself. He might say "bairn" and then change the word to the standard "born." Also, "anymore they don't call it 'teaberry'; they call it 'wintergreen.'" Or, "they don't call them 'panthers' now like we did; they call them 'mountain lions.'" Wanting to please, he courteously defers to visitors. If he sees a frown as he talks, he knows his speech has gone over the head of his guest. At such times, as a good host, he tries to find the "proper" way to say a thing. Each time he does this, he sacrifices a bit of poetic freedom and edges nearer the ordinary.

His eloquence draws from the rhetoric that influenced him as a child — utterances that mystically stayed with him long after others ceased to say "odd gosh" and "yander." These exotic words were still spoken when he was a child, but they are not evident among Ray's own offspring, who have moved away and live in contemporary society.

"They are coming from 'Natural Geogravity' to 'camera' me," Ray says. And, "It 'suffers' me to see so many young people on drugs." His neighbors either accept his speech differences or do not perceive them, but to them he is as hypnotic as he is to outsiders.

For a scholar who might wish to edit Ray's mountain speech, the job is difficult. Like most mountaineers, he speaks for effect, using the language in whatever way will best fix the proper image in a listener's mind. He might in the same sentence say "ain't" and "hain't" or "it" and "hit." Other times he might say "plowing" in one sentence and "a-plowing" in another. There are times when the "g" is left off the ending of a word like "going," and other times it is there.

Soon I decide that it is best not to note every detail of Ray Hicks's language,

The Valley of the River

just as an illustrator does not draw a model's every feature in a portrait—such as lines between the teeth. To be slavish in detail of speech, I discover, is to lose the essence, the beauty, and the meanings in Ray Hicks's strange dialogue. Nor can one feel the enchantment simply by reading his words. One must sit before him in his old parlor, hear the resonance in his speech, see the flame in his eyes, watch the impassioned gestures of his great hands.

As months pass, I often return to the rustic house on Old Mountain Road to dig deeper into Ray Hicks's past, to laugh at his humor, to hear his songs of another time, to listen to him play a German harmonica given to him in his youth.

On a Christmas Eve, the roads are covered with snow and ice. Two of our daughters, Lyn and Eden, have come to spend the holidays at our mountain home; daughter Andrea is expected by nightfall. In the afternoon, Lyn and I pack my wife Fran's truffles and chess tarts—our holiday gifts to the Hickses—and we set out on the forty-minute drive to the Hicks place. We expect to drop off the gifts and return home directly to avoid a new cover of snow. Lyn, a teacher and longtime devotee of Shakespeare and British literature, has become interested in the Hickses through my letters. She wants to meet them and does not mind that there might be trouble getting to their house.

We arrive in midafternoon to find Ray, Rosa, and Ted alone; but soon the visit turns festive. Ray begins spinning stories, and Rosa coaxes him to bring out his old harmonica. Two couples from nearby farms drop by, but Ray has often talked and played for them before. Lyn, however, is a new convert, so Ray cheerfully neglects the other guests. From time to time Rosa leaves off talking with the guests and requests a song from Ray. "Play 'Old Molly Hare,'" she says. "Now, play the one you made up about the little old railroad."

The afternoon rushes by and the thermometer plummets as darkness nears. Finally I am able to get the message across that Lyn and I are expected for dinner at home, that we must go before new ice covers the roads. Then Rosa goes into the kitchen and returns with a bunch of galax leaves, a sack of dried apples, and a head of cabbage—her Yule gifts to Fran.

On the slippery, narrow road home, Lyn sits in silence as the car's headlights play over myriad Christmas-card scenes. Presently she begins to talk of Ray from her own scholarly perspective. To her, she says, he is a Homer, or perhaps one of the ancient tellers of Beowulf; he is a throwback, never to be found again.

The Valley of the River

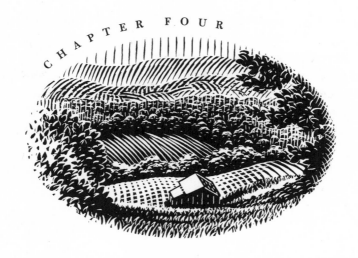
Young Years on Old Mountain Road

Ray was the fourth of Nathan and Rena Hicks's children; he began early to ingest the wisdom and ways of his pioneer kinfolk.

Father Nathan's parents, Benjamin and Julie, lived a half-mile away, at the end of Old Mountain Road, and little Ray walked to see them in every day of good weather. He was their companion and pet, the center of their home. For them he cheerfully fetched water from the spring, chopped kindling with a dull axe, and swept the yard with a small straw broom Benjamin made for him. When there were beans to shell, he would sit with his grandmother and listen to her bewitching stories and ballads. It was with Julie and Benjamin—even more than with his parents—that his fascination for word and song began.

On winter evenings by the mudrock fireplace, Ray listened to Benjamin's ghost stories and cradled them in his memory. Long before starting to school he could sing ballads and call up old narratives. To Benjamin and Julie, the light-haired child was a wonder, a gift of God, and they showered him with the lore of ages past.

Ray saw this kindly and ramrod-straight grandfather as fearless. Accounts of Benjamin's life left their mark. All the Hickses knew about the infant Benjamin and the bald eagle. When Benjamin's mother Rebecca helped her husband with the crops in summer, she would fold baby Benjamin in a wrapper and lay him in the shade of trees at the edge of the field. One warm day as she hoed corn on new ground, a thing happened that awed and terrified her. Within her view, a great eagle swept down to the clearing's edge and upon the sleeping baby. Rebecca dropped her hoe and ran screaming toward the spot as the bird sank its talons into the baby's wrapper. Hearing her shouts from the far end of the field, husband Samuel came running. Alarmed by the approaching parents, the eagle let go of the baby and flew away. Benjamin slept through it all—the noise of the eagle's tearing at the wrapper and the shrieks of his mother.

His family's frequent retelling of the story elevated Ray's grandfather to mythical heights. Even after Ray had grown taller than Benjamin, he held his grandfather in awe.

"Yiah, I can go show you the piece of ground today," says Ray "Right down yander is where it was. Growed up now, where it was once a field. But that eagle they called the bald could carry babies up to two years old. They had pictures in a book, pictures of an eagle like that going with a baby—flying with the baby hanging down in a wrapper. Drawed a picture. In our school books. Had it pictured."

For years after he heard the story, the boy Ray would look to the skies. He rarely saw an eagle, but there would be hawks wheeling above, looking for mice, voles, shrews, fledgling birds, even rabbits. When once he saw a hawk flying with a long, stringy, dark object hanging from its beak, he ran to his grandmother. "She told me it was a hawk with a snake. They'll do that, a hawk will. They'll fetch snakes and fly up and take them to their young'uns. Created to do that."

From the old people—grandparents on both sides—Ray learned stories of the Holy Bible, but it was his mother, Rena, who taught him most about God and religion. Taking him by the hand on Sunday mornings, she'd walk several miles to a Primitive Baptist Church. There she'd leave cabbages or potatoes or canned fruit on a bench at the church's entry.

"Why do you do that?" Ray asked his mother. She told him that the food was for the "bishop" (as local congregations often called their clergyman) and his wife and children. Says Ray: "The reason they didn't raise their own vittles like everybody else was that they didn't have time. You see, bishops moved from one meetinghouse to another. Most of them didn't light in one place like us;

they'd ride horses or mules from way off. Mama and them couldn't afford to pay the bishop in legal; they'd have to bring food. Called it a pounding."

Poundings were meant for resident preachers also. A bishop who elected to live in the vicinity was cherished. Settlers built his home, carried firewood to his hearth, left him cabbage and potatoes, and took him healing herbs in times of sickness. He was the center of respect in the world of Beech Mountain, a man close to God, an eloquent, knowing man who helped succor families when there was need.

Many preachers had fewer belongings than the members of their congregations; because money was scarce, the offering plate was unknown in some churches. Although Rena Hicks admired her preacher, she could not give money.

If a clergyman came to visit, a poor family might bring out the best of their hoarded goods—a cured ham, strings of jerky, or choice preserved foods; they were honored to have a man of God at their tables or under their roofs for a night. Yet there were times when a visit might not have been fully welcome.

One raw, leaden day when Ray and grandfather Benjamin sat by the fire, they heard from outside a halloo above the chilly wind. Benjamin went quickly to the porch and hailed his visitor, a lame and aging preacher driving a donkey-pulled buggy.

Ray says that as his grandfather strode up the knoll he shouted back that he was going to help the parson. Then he greeted the preacher cordially and servilely. He knew the visitor feared the donkey might run down the hill and wreck the buggy, so Benjamin tied the animal to a tree and then stepped inside the shafts and eased the rig slowly to the house.

The wind blew hard out of the northwest, and the preacher welcomed the cozy inside. Benjamin invited him to freshen up with kettle-heated water. As the guest removed his boots and bathed his feet, Benjamin hurried to the kitchen to boil coffee. Although brown sugar was hard to come by, Benjamin decided to pull down the precious luxury from the cupboard. At that moment Julie entered and, as she removed her wraps, spied the brown sugar her husband was about to ladle into a cup. Already she had seen the donkey tied at the top of the hill and the buggy standing by the porch. She knew the preacher had arrived, so she rushed over and placed a hand over the mouth of the sugar jar.

"Her eyes sparked," says Ray, "and she told my grandpa that she pulled galax way up on the mountain for two days. Said, 'That's what half a jar of sugar cost me: two days' work away from the house. And you're about to hand it to the preacher. My sugar. Him eating it up. If he needs sugar so bad, let him go pull galax like I did.' "

Benjamin screwed the lid back on, put the sugar away, and took unsweetened coffee to the minister. Later they all ate ham and eggs, but Julie had drawn the line against guests, even the bishop, eating her precious brown sugar.

In Ray's early life, church was a wonderment. He sat on the edge of the hard benches and relished the flowery preaching; he sang shrilly when the congregation sang. Years later he would recall those times:

"Ye gods! You talk about feeling. If their songs didn't make you feel good, nothing could. If they didn't make something come on, nobody else needn't try. A *feeling* there. You could tell by their eyes that they was a-feeling with the spirit of God."

Little Ray would join the clapping and shouting when the preacher kindled the gathering to a pitch of ecstasy. The rejoicing would begin in the middle of the sermon. "Each person'd be a-singing a different song to the praising of God. With them singing with the words mixed up, it'd make your hair stand on your neck," Ray recalls. "Gah, I never forget the way they sang different words and different tunes at the same time. Somehow all that difference made up a song of its own."

There were no hymnbooks. Songs were pulled from memory, and if a word or two was missed, the fevered singing did not suffer.

Few churches of the settlement were so liberal as to allow musical instruments. Congregations often sang their tunes in minor keys, without accompaniment. Their ascetic ways were much like those of the Amish and Quakers of the Pennsylvania country from which so many had migrated. To them church was serious. Members sang mournful and God-praising melodies in which they often pictured themselves as sinful and unworthy.

"Mama said we were 'Prims,' and one Sunday, walking to church, I asked her what was a Prim.

" 'It's somebody who's a Primitive Baptist,' she told me. See, they sprung off from old regular Baptists, the Baptists who claim to be with history, you know. One bunch split from them and made themselves Hardshell Baptists. Hardshell. It means they's so hard to change on their belief of the Bible. And then later the Primitive Baptists split up with the Hardshell. And Mama told me when I got old enough to be baptized, the bishop wouldn't sprinkle me like the

Presbyterians do. To be saved, you got to be mired in water like Jesus was. Go down in water and back out. Dip down and back out."

Later, Rena left the Prims. It was a Presbyterian preacher's strange vision that caused her to change her lifelong allegiance. The story goes that as the preacher slept one frigid January night, he dreamed of snow mounting in high drifts, isolating a frightened mother and her hungry children. Into the next day the vision haunted him, and he began to ponder who could be in trouble. As late afternoon came on and snow buried the roads beneath Beech Mountain, he recalled that Nathan Hicks, who lived far out on Old Mountain Road, was away from home, probably far from his family. Perhaps the dream had meaning.

He thought it foolish to act upon a fantasy, but the vision persisted. At last he loaded provisions in his old Plymouth and set out for the Hicks home. He knew the way, because on every other Sunday of passable weather, he drove this same route from Banner Elk, across Lee Gwaltney Road and over the rough approaches of Devil's Highway and Andy Hicks Road. His destination was a patch of woods well south of the Hicks home. There, according to Ray, he conducted a "grove" service. Such a meeting got its name, Ray says, because it was staged in a clearing in the woods. As yet, there was no Presbyterian meetinghouse, and some worshipers met there because they were displeased by a split in their former Primitive Baptist Church.

Ray explains further: "They sawed off two chestnut saplings and nailed a board on them to make a pulpit. A place to hold his Bible, you know. Called it a grove meeting. And Mama'd go there when the old Primitive Baptist split up. That's how he got to know us. Name was Pritchard. From Banner Elk. Came every other Sunday."

When finally the minister arrived at the Old Mountain Road home of the Hickses, he found his vision had directed him to the right family; Rena and the children had eaten their last food two nights before. Rena thought that perhaps the blizzard had kept Nathan away, and her face was swollen from crying. In icy bedrooms, the smallest of her children shivered in their featherbeds. Ray, who was older, was up and about; he comforted his mother the best he knew how.

The minister had brought bread, milk, and canned food. By the light of an oil lamp and in the warmth of the kitchen, Rena, the preacher, and the children feasted happily.

"Later, Mama wrote the bishop that if his church would have her, she wanted to be a Presbyterian."

Young Years on Old Mountain Road

Preacherfolk and the gentle Renas of the past joined to bring order to wilderness life. In the shadows of Beech Mountain, ministerial rhetoric and the instincts of women had always calmed their free-spirited men infinitely better than laws. Churches on these stretched borders of civilization seemed to control the rustic adventurers better than sheriffs or jails. Community life grew up around meetinghouses, and many neighbors buckled under the fire-and-brimstone morality of preachers.

"Now, Pritchard, he preached at them grove meetings for a few years more," says Ray. "Then he got started with the church, got to getting him some lumber, and we's a few years a-building that church. One part would nearly rot before we got the other part built. What was so bad about it, your joists, your ceiling joists, would be on there, and the sun [was] a-drawing that lumber and the rain'd hit it, and it drawed it out and swelled it in the belly. In the middle of the wall. Finally, we got it covered with shingles, just like this house had, and kept on; it was several years before it got done. I worked on it.

"You know," Ray goes on, "as they teached us, they'd keep us scared of the Roman Catholics." To him and those about him, the deep conflicts of the kings and peoples of long-past history were unknown; but the mistily recalled myths of Catholic influences on their pioneer ancestors filtered down. Ray and the children of the twentieth century were afraid of the pope's followers, who, they thought, would "cut y'r head off if you disobeyed them; just cut y'r head off." Because elders would tell such stories with firm conviction, the little boy Ray "was mightily scared" of Catholics—people he never once encountered in the mountains.

By the time Ray came along, religion in the hills had spread to encompass many forms. Settlers and itinerant preachers together fomented new beliefs as their stories bridged generations much in the way of the ancient tribal Israelites.

Besides being the centers of spiritual life, the churches on the slopes of Beech served their communities in mundane ways. At meetinghouses, settlers saw remote neighbors, learned local gossip, gleaned news of the outside world, formed quilting bees, and traded ways to plant and harvest crops. Variously they stomped, clapped, and shouted—much to the glee of little Ray Hicks. In a few churches, fiddles or pump organs were actually played. Worshipers could let off steam built up by the day-to-day intensity of their hard lives. To many pioneers, this was a way to show love for a higher power.

Benjamin and Julie Hicks shared their mountains with the birds, the animals, the forests, and the plants; they sowed seeds and watched in awe as tendrils pushed through the soft mountain earth. They saw the sun rise and set of a day, and they looked on all this magic as "God's way." They believed that nature evolved from a heavenly mystery too deep to understand.

Ray learned early from his grandparents that nobody understands all things, that every creature must have faith in something it does not comprehend:

"Now you take that little wren in its nest. It's got God in it, just like people has, but the wren don't deny it, don't think nothing about it. Just goes on its way building its nest, bringing up its young'uns and teaching them to fly. Did you ever see the wrens just before their young'uns fly? They get out there in the air and fly by the nest, over and over, so the little'uns can get the hang of it. See? That's God in them. Nobody teached them little birds how to do that.

"I saw that when I was out working the taters and in the woods looking for galax. I saw it was a wonderful life. Now I was too young to join the church, but I didn't have to join to believe in God.

"God was in me just like he was in the wrens."

Ray learned that hard and constant work would be his life, and he steeled himself against want; but often he felt small prejudices, even within his own family:

"What we had at home was good, but there was never enough. When the preacher or kinfolks came to dinner, us kids didn't get to eat. We was dressed so bad that Mama didn't want company to see us. She'd shoo us outside and we'd just go hungry."

Ray thought this unjust; guests should not be asked to stay if they were going to eat food meant for the children. He sometimes complained:

"How come, Bessie?" he asked. "Every time people come, Mama uses the wood I chopped to cook the vittles; but you and me and the others don't get to eat."

Like animals and birds and fish that occupy nearly all their time in search of food, Ray and his brothers and sisters would savor the plainest edible thing so long as it filled their bellies. In winter they gathered nuts and ate raw turnips and rutabagas out of the fields. In summer they picked blackberries, huckleberries, and wild salad greens. In the fall, apples came in, and they ate squirrel and rabbit stews. Often hungry, they took delight in simple and meager foods. Ray grew to manhood before he ever saw a fat person.

Young Years on Old Mountain Road

Until the end of his life, great-grandfather Samuel made shoes for the Hicks brood. Long after he died, his progeny would laugh about a joking promise he made to Blind Rollie.

Ray remembers: "Now Blind Rollie wuddn't plumb blind, and I'd meet him sometimes, me going to the little grist mill. His eyes looked white like a blind person. He could run fast and he had heel irons on his old shoes, and on that old mountain road down yander and hit dark or late in the evening, you'd look and see sparks a-flying, hitting the rocks. Old Blind Rollie, you know."

In the story the Hickses tell, Blind Rollie kept begging Samuel to give him a pair of shoes, the very shoes Samuel wore. At last Samuel gave in; he promised that when he died he'd leave his shoes to Blind Rollie.

"So now Samuel got sick," says Ray. "And old Blind Rollie—lived across there in a old house—would come by every day and say, 'Is Uncle Sam, my buddywoo, is he dead yet?' 'No, Blind Rollie,' they'd say. 'Sam ain't dead yet.'"

Grandmother Julie and mother Rena fashioned the clothes Ray and his brothers and sisters wore, cutting and sewing cloth into overalls and dresses. Julie could find no one to fix her broken spinning wheel, so the device stood in the corner as a reminder of her childhood. She twisted wool with her fingers, just as the ancients did. From her small herd of sheep she and her granddaughter Viola, along with young Ray, gathered shearing; they tore it apart, washed and dried it, and she made yarn from it. When Julie had twisted enough yarn, she knitted stockings and sweaters for the family. In the winter after Ray turned five, Julie knitted the boy two pairs of stockings.

"She fretted about us young'uns, Grandma Julie did," said Ray. "I remember her telling Viola one time. She said, 'Viola, I hope Nathan can get enough legal to shoe Ray and the other young'uns this winter.' She was afraid the stockings she made us wouldn't be no good without good shoes."

Ray thinks his father gave much of himself to provide for the family. From spring to fall, Nathan labored for fifty cents a day on the larger farms along the Watauga River. When he was not working for wages, he plowed, hoed, and harvested his own land. Also, he would go onto Beech Mountain and over to Dark Ridge to pull herbs and cut haw.

One morning Ray's father talked to Rena before setting off for Banner Elk. "He told Mama that them steers of ours was too slow. He said we'd need mules to pull the sled to market. So he took all he'd saved to buy them two mules.

"Mama told him us young'uns would be a-needing shoes for school, and said Dad'd have to pay taxes and pay back Mister Mast for last spring's fertilizer.

"Dad said that was a chance he had to take. Said them mules could haul taters and cabbage to market, and one of 'em could pull the sled up on the mountain where he'd load it with 'sang and haw. Said more could be put on that sled than he could carry on his back. Said the mules could help us get back our savings."

When Nathan brought home the mules, called Zeb and Nick, little Ray was proud. He learned to stay away from the ornery Zeb, but he found Nick docile and fond of being rubbed and petted. Ray would walk under the kindly mule and pat its belly and flanks.

Some days the fickle mountain weather would not permit outdoor work; at those times Nathan might play his dulcimer. Young Ray would hear the music and come sit with his father on the long porch. From Benjamin and Julie and from Rena's parents — Andrew Jackson and Suzy Ann, also named Hicks — the boy had learned the melodies and lyrics of many ballads.

"He'd tell me, Dad would, 'Come sing for me, Ray.' He'd be a-strumming his dulcimer, you know, and he'd say, 'Come sing "Omie Wise" and I'll help ye.'"

Ray liked to sing, and Nathan, who never seemed to remember the lyrics, delighted in hearing his son's high-pitched voice. He knew, too, that Ray kept in his small head a storehouse of ballads.

In late summer of 1928 Nathan and Ray hiked over Beech Mountain to Heaton's Store, across the road from the Elk River. There the two sang and played by the roadside, and a few travelers between Roan Mountain and Banner Elk stopped to listen and throw small coins into a hat. The Heaton venture was not a failure, but it was not worth doing again. Still, it gave Nathan ideas. Next time, he figured, they would go to Boone, the busiest place he knew. The pair would go on a Saturday when the streets were crowded; if they took in enough money, they would eat at a real café.

Ray counted the days until the morning when Nathan placed him on Nick's back. The journey to Boone would be longer than that to Heaton, but by riding the gentle Nick, the pair would find the trip easier, and they would arrive fresh. Nathan explained to Ray that he would lead Nick across the mountains and they would arrive in Boone by the time the shops opened.

Young Years on Old Mountain Road

The only leather remaining on the boy's shoe tops were the cups over his toes; he held the shoes on his feet by gripping them with his turned-in toes. But when Nathan lifted him up onto the mule, the shoes fell off, and Nathan gathered them up and handed them, with the dulcimer, to his son. Then he led off on foot, with Ray happily astride the mule.

Ray says he and his father—riding a mule and carrying a dulcimer and an old pair of shoes—must have been an odd sight as they rode onto King Street in the heart of Boone. Near Farmers Hardware they stopped and hitched Nick to a post. Then Nathan placed his hat on the sidewalk and Ray slipped his feet into the dilapidated shoes.

On the street corner, Nathan played the dulcimer lustily; Ray's small but strident voice sang out over the competing sounds of the village. Within minutes, the Saturday people gathered. Ray sang ballads like "John Henry," "The Brown Girl," "Omie Wise," and "The Willow Garden." Coins were thrown into the hat, and wagons and old cars stopped and clogged the thoroughfare. Drivers got out of their vehicles and shoppers filled the sidewalk.

"They wanted to know where we came from, them people did. Asked things like, 'How can I get one of them [dulcimers]?'"

Nathan's hunch was right. Nickels, dimes, even quarters rang into the hat. When people found that Nathan had made the instrument himself, a few placed orders for dulcimers of their own. Nathan smiled broadly. He and Ray would come to town every Saturday. Maybe he would bring his banjo, too.

But as father and son performed, one policeman was joined by another, each trying to unsnarl the jam of horses, mules, wagons, buggies, and old cars. King Street began to look like a cattle auction, and the policemen at last despaired. Ray recounts that one of them came over to Nathan and told him: "Mister Hicks, we cannot handle this traffic any longer. You're going to have to take your git-tar, or whatever that is, and go home. If you come back again a-singing and a-playing on this street, we'll have to put you in jail."

The rough-hewn troubadours gathered their coins, and Nathan lifted Ray onto the mule. Into his bib pockets he stuffed a few addresses, in his side pockets he pushed down coins, and Ray cradled more change in his father's upturned hat. Now Nathan climbed up on the mule, and people on the sidewalks stopped and watched as the father and boy rode bareback slowly along King Street. The son held his father's hat and the battered shoes. Nathan rested the strange musical instrument in the crook of his burly arm.

Young Years on Old Mountain Road

After stopping to eat, they rode on to the outskirts, where Nathan dismounted and led old Nick on foot. Along the way, crossing Valle Mountain, Ray recalls, they cheerfully sang tunes like "Fly Around My Pretty Little Miss, Fly Around My Daisy." Women and men working in the fields and carrying water from wells waved happily to the robust father and his young son.

Although he and the boy never again performed on the sidewalks of Boone, Nathan obtained enough orders for dulcimers to pay his taxes and redeem the credit ticket carried at Mast's Store.

One morning Ray arose and could not find his old shoes. In the night Nathan had taken them from beneath his bed and had hidden them in the hollow of a tree.

Later Ray found the shoes and began wearing them again. He went down to the barn where his father was working and begged to be put on Nick; when Nathan picked up the boy, the shoes fell off. This time Nathan put them away so that Ray was not able to find them.

"I guess he knowed they's a-ruining my toes."

On another day, Nathan was hooking Zeb and Nick to his sled; when he hit the traces, the cantankerous Zeb kicked suddenly, and both hoofs grazed Nathan's head. The blow sheared off a shock of hair at the scalp and embedded it in the barn's weatherboarding. The hair remained there until one spring a decade later, when chipping sparrows plucked it out and took it to cushion their nests.

These were by no means days of plenty in Ray's young life, but they were the easiest he was ever to see. He would not begin school until fall, and he was still too young for heavy chores. The tasks he did—chopping wood, sweeping porches, shelling beans, singing for his father—were not strenuous. As he performed them, he told over to himself the stories he had learned and sang ballads to the wind. He lived close to nature in an existence filled with hardships, but his thoughts, stimulated by the tales and songs, ranged freely.

Nathan and Rena raised turkeys to sell at Thanksgiving, and the birds roamed all over their acres. One day they assigned to Ray the chore of keeping the turkeys off neighboring properties. He became the shepherd and the turkeys his sheep. He would lie on the hillside and think about the ways of birds and animals. He would ponder their place in "God's creation" and their often unnoticed habits. He called baby turkeys and chickens "diddles," and he studied how they related to their mothers. They grew up with the sameness of a group, but often the behavior of one diddle might be different from that of the rest.

"Turkeys and chickens was once wild," Ray says. "Everything we've got was once wild that God created here—people and all. Wild. With that wild nature, the way all was created. And so with the chicken hens that Mama kept. I would watch them. Other kids wasn't interested in that; they played 'whoopy hide' and them other games. But I liked the games that was created wild. It must have been [meant] for it to be kept in me—for the purpose I'm a-living now. To help others. Maybe that's supposed to be kept in me.

"And so these chicken hens, now, with their little diddles. One . . . like young'uns . . . one will want to be petted more than others; want its mother to look a little more on it. And all of them would come when it'd start raining. Hit'd get cold and them little diddles would run and get under their mama's feathers. When they got bigger they'd come a-running and get under her. They'd be so big then that they'd lift the mama hen off the ground. And she'd try to hold them and they'd carry her off.

"Now the mother would peck the diddles to wean them, to be light with them, not reign them in too heavy. To punish them she'd catch their bill and twist it. If she had to peck any one diddle three times, it meant she was through with it; the diddle was on its own. Time to make a living on its own.

"Now some young'uns, seems like they don't want to grow up like that diddle. And some mamas don't want to wean them, seems like."

Ray thought that animals were not unlike human beings: "Mama hens maybe raised their diddles better than human mothers look after theirs, sometimes.

"Like one time I went a-visiting with my mama, over yander across Beech Creek, and this fellow—a lot older than me—come in to where his mama set. Said he wanted money. Said he was going to a molasses boil. Wanted a dime. His mama said she was busy. 'Just wait.' But he said, 'Well, where's your pocketbook? I can go get it.' Well, the mama wasn't thinking too well, and she said, 'It's in the little back room in there.' And the boy took off and went to it. But when she heard him unsnap the purse, she got up and went running in there. She didn't think he'd find her pocketbook, you know. She went in there and grabbed her purse and yelled, 'You ain't a-seeing what I got in my purse.' Then she got him out a dime. Now if she hadn't gone in there, he might have taken a quarter. See, his mama hadn't twisted his bill like mine had. I was teached to hang together with love. I'd never take my mama's money. Money was too hard to get, and Mama had teached us we was on our own."

As Rena's chickens grew, Ray saw that the too-dependent diddle—finally spurned by its mother—was at first lost. But as it grew it toughened up and "got in with the others"; it would sometimes join in playing and fighting, but Ray saw that it was no longer part of the group. It roamed the fields and made its own way.

"The others'd stay together to protect theirselves. They'd play games—run to see which could catch a grasshopper first. Hungry. Then a little snake'd run out. Maybe the snake'd be too big for one diddle to swallow, but the diddle would try. It'd swallow the snake down its craw, always take a snake tail first, and the snake would come back up, its head sticking out. Another diddle would grab the snake's head and pull it out. Then the others'd come and they'd peck away on it until the little snake was gone.

"Now the diddle that the mama had twisted its beak, it growed up to be smarter than the others, because it had to go on its own first. The mama had put it out to keep it from bothering her. That diddle got tough and learned about life. 'Cause it was on its own, it survived when the foxes come one night and eat the others.

"God learned it to save the seed, teached the diddle how to survive."

Little Ray observed that the chickens were smarter than turkeys. "I learnt that from watching Mama's chickens. I saw that they was a difference between chickens and turkeys. See, like them shepherds in Bible times, I studied ever one of them; they was all different. But, now, chickens don't always run in flocks like turkeys. I had to stay with the turkeys. Keep them off the neighbors' land. Drive them to their roosts at night. Chickens was smarter.

"Now that same little chicken I spoke about—hit growed up to be a rooster. Got grown. Hit's out in the woods, in the thicket, a white laurel patch . . . "

Here Ray pauses and grins: "Now from here on out, you know, this story ain't for real. But it'll be better if you pretend like it is.

"Well, see, the rooster was crowing away when a fox came in on it. Rooster. A-crowing.

Young Years on Old Mountain Road

"Boy, it was a beautiful morning. Clear. The sun a-shining bright. The fox said, 'Gah, that crowing sounded so good.' Said, 'Rooster, raise one foot and then crow.' So that rooster felt big; he helt his foot up and went, 'Rick, a-rick, rick, a-rick, a-roo.' Then the fox said, 'Oh, that *did* have a whing to it. That's it. Said, 'Now see if you can crow with one foot up and one eye shut.' So that rooster got to feeling a little bigger. He raised his foot up and shut his left eye. He went, 'Rick, a-rick, a-roo. Rick, a-rick, a-roo.' And the fox said, 'Gah, now *that* did it.' Said, 'Now see if you can shut both eyes and one foot up.' This is the same diddle, now, on its own. And it was now a rooster. It raised one foot but kept one eye just a little open, and the fox didn't know it. See, that rooster trained hisself. Had to leave and go on its own, remember? Couldn't stay with the other chickens. And hit'd learned life, the life of a chicken, just like we'd learned God's life of a human being. That rooster knowed! Kept that eye open a little bit. Then he crowed again: 'Rick, a-rick, a-rick, a-rick, a-roo.' And the fox jumped at him! Well, the rooster just flipped and flew up on a tree limb — just high enough that the fox couldn't reach it — his tongue a-hanging out, wanting to eat the rooster so bad.

"The rooster yelled down, 'Rick, a-rick, a-rick, a-roo. You fooled me but then I fooled you.'"

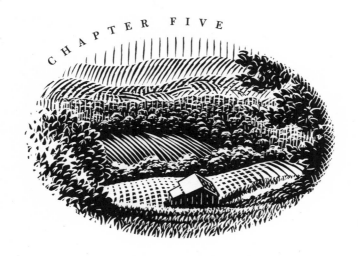

CHAPTER FIVE

Hard Times on Pickbritches Creek

In 1929, the year Ray Hicks turned seven, his father bought a stand of black birch trees along a valley stream called Pickbritches Creek, so named because blackberry and other briar bushes grew along its banks. From here it was a foot-weary journey to the homeplace on Old Mountain Road, even if one cut across fields and meadows, so Nathan set up crude housekeeping in an abandoned sawmill shack. He told his family to expect a turnabout in their lives; he would pay for the tract with cash earned by distilling oil from birch wood.

"He told Mama that the land was cheap, because of the birch trees," Ray recalls. "See, them birches was about the only tree up there that the lumber company didn't want. They took out the good wood—the pine and oak and hickory—and left just the birches." But Nathan reasoned he could distill oil from the birch wood in the same way he made teaberry oil; both oils were used for flavoring—teaberry for chewing gum, birch for candy. "Dad told us a man over in Tennessee would buy all the oil he could make, he'd pick it up at Dad's still."

Rena had misgivings. She wondered how Nathan could live in a sawmill shack with nobody to cook for him and do his washing. But Nathan had an answer: "He told Mama that soon as he set up his still, he'd send for me'n Mae, a sister that was older than me. Mae would cook on an old stove the loggers had left. He wanted me to keep him company, sing songs with him at nights. He told Mama that he'd make enough in legal to build a house up near Beaverdam. Said, 'It won't be long. I'll come get you and the young'uns, and we'll just rent out the place here.'"

The arrangement still did not appeal to Rena, but she acquiesced; she knew more than anyone else how hard her muscular, sad-eyed husband worked and how he ached for a better life.

On an early November morning, when snow patches lay on the ground, Nathan packed the distillery into his sled and led the mules, Zeb and Nick, on a long trek to the banks of Pickbritches Creek. The next day he returned to Old Mountain Road and fetched daughter Mae, son Ray, and their belongings.

The trio settled down in the sawmill shack, where they hung bed sheets for partitions. Mae prepared meals on a small, rickety stove, and Ray tasted his new freedom alone; he often roamed the placid vale beneath Stone Mountain. Here, out of earshot of his father and the workers at the still, he delved into his unusual imagination. Even so early, he showed the gift of invention, of memory, of tongue, as he recited aloud the stories learned from the old people of the Hicks clan. He happily awaited Sunday afternoons, when his handsome father — dressed in clean shirt, tie, overalls, and suit jacket — strolled with him over the hills and through the forests. There Nathan would identify herbs and roots; he taught the boy how to survive when lost in the mountain wilderness.

"He'd tell me stories," Ray remembers. "Tell me something funny to make me laugh; he wanted me — a little old boy, you know — to stay with him. Wanted me to be happy there."

One blue-skied Sunday the following May they strolled into a beautiful valley. Leisure hours with his son would relax Nathan after a strenuous week. ("Gah, he worked so hard; sweat pouring out of him.") He knew the land they walked upon could be bought, and he dreamed of how he might become wealthy.

Returning from their hike up the valley, Nathan and Ray stopped at two large clumps of rotting brush, the only blemish in the whole valley. In his mind, Nathan had already assumed ownership of the adjoining property. He thought the debris should be cleared away, and with his foot he raked aside a small pile which he would set ablaze; if it burned slowly, he would ignite the larger piles. From his coat pocket he pulled out a long kitchen match that the wind blew out instantly.

"Too bad to let this mess stay," he said. "But we'll let it be; that was my only match."

Leaving the small pile, he fished absently through his pockets and by chance discovered a short match, one he had whittled for a toothpick. The stem was so short that when he scratched its head across his overalls a flame shot out and nipped his fingers; reflexively he dropped the match, and it fell upon the largest pile of tinder.

"Gah, the fire took off," Ray remembers. "The brush was old and dry and spunky. Dad was cussing and stomping, but when he'd put out the fire in one place, it'd break out in another. It was a-popping and a-cracking and Dad was yelling at me to get back."

Nathan tried to isolate the blaze by kicking dirt around its base. Containing it briefly, he ripped off his jacket, his only one, and beat upon the erupted heaps. Driven back by the intense heat, he tore off a low-hanging hemlock limb and raked the surrounding soil upon the edges of the fire. Still the blaze leaped higher.

"It was a-building its own wind," Ray said, "and it started catching the other heap."

A wind swept from across the valley into the faces of the two.

" 'Get back,' Dad yelled. 'It's gonna be a wildfire.' "

No single man could fight the blaze now. So Nathan picked up his son and ran with him to an old path on the edge of the valley. In the past the trail had been used to haul lumber on a steel-wheeled tram.

Hoisting Ray upon the road, apparently away from the spreading fire, Nathan cried to him above the roar: " 'You stay up here,' he told me. Said, 'If the wind comes at you, get away, but stay on the tram road.' Said he'd find me."

Nathan left on the run. He would try to find farmers to help, those who lived along Pickbritches Creek; failing that he'd run all the way to Beaverdam Church and interrupt morning services.

A sunny day had turned woeful, and Ray whimpered, worrying more for his father's safety than for the burning valley.

"I was on the tram road, away from the fire, but the smoke would come and go. Clear up a little and here it'd come again. Choked me sometimes and I'm 'way back there."

In fear he stood watching the wildfire. Suddenly something struck him violently from behind, a blow so powerful that the boy was knocked clean off the

Hard Times on Pickbritches Creek

roadstead and down the hill. Dazed and frightened, he struggled to his feet and looked back to see the thing that had hit him:

"Somebody's old cow."

The animal, so blinded by the smoke that it had not seen Ray, ran crazily down the path, stumbling over crossties. Ray watched in pain and shock as the cow careened along the road into another roiling screen of smoke.

"She was a-running with her hair afire. Went on down the trail with her tail a-waving and fire a-shooting out of it. I guess I would have learned later if she'd got burnt up. But nobody around ever mentioned it. She ran down there to the creek to get in it and put the fire out."

Ray sat down on an oak log and waited for his head to clear and for the ache in his shoulders to go away. He watched as a groundhog lumbered from its hole and scampered off. He saw chipmunks racing about and chattering; they seemed to be scolding him for bringing the fire.

In the mountains, the month of May often comes before new grass grows and tree buds appear. This year winter had lingered, and the spreading fire was unimpeded by the normal moist green of spring. The blaze roared across the gray, dry carpet of last year's grass and up the bare trees. Ray watched the flames eat into the forest and skip across the arid field. He moved down the tram road to be away from the expanding hell, but the smoke thickened.

Ray thought that by now Nathan would have found help, but, with the smoke and heat building around him, he still saw no sign of his father. Soon hot gusts enveloped the boy, and he wandered about, now off the tram; it flashed into his mind that perhaps he should take flight to Mae and the shack. Then he stopped to think: Dad might come back and I'll be gone. He'll forget putting out the fire and come looking for me. I ought to stay here.

But terror grew within him, and he thought that, after all, it might be better to run. He recalled that his father had told him to move away from the smoke if it reached the tram road; flames now licked the edges of this same ground.

Fresh winds swept toward him from across the valley. He could reason no more and yielded to instinct. Turning in his path, the boy ran fast against the winds, into the familiar, cool mountain air, away from the encroaching firestorm and toward home.

When finally he came to a safe place on a hillock, he turned and looked back at the dark horror; unashamedly he cried to see the destruction, because he knew that his father and the volunteers could not cope with the raging inferno.

Hard Times on Pickbritches Creek

Breathing hard, he collapsed on the dry grass and rested. His lungs ached, his small legs quivered, his eyes burned.

Hours had passed since Nathan and Ray had left on their walk. When the two did not return for a hot dinner, Mae paced about worrying. As the afternoon passed, she smelled smoke and went outside to see the gathering dark skies. Though alarmed, she knew her father to be woodswise and resourceful; he would not let little Ray or himself be harmed. When at last she spotted Ray approaching through a clump of hickory saplings, she ran toward him. They met in the clearing, and she grabbed and tightly hugged the grimy-faced child.

It was a long while before the boy could speak, but he nodded when his sister asked if Nathan was safe. Together they waited through the daylight hours, and toward evening the sky lightened. When at last the sun sank beyond the distant Tennessee peaks, they saw deep orange and blood-red streaks in the heavens. Although the sky was still draped with smoke from the valley, it was evident by the waning glow off low-lying clouds that Nathan and the farmers were gaining on the runaway blaze.

Evening came on with a chill, a small blessing for the overwrought battlers, but it was midnight before the exhausted, sweaty, and begrimed Nathan dragged himself into the shack. He flung himself down upon a cot and for long moments said nothing. Nor did Mae and Ray ask questions; they would let their father recover first. After dozing, he at last pulled himself up and asked for a dipper of cool water.

" 'I knew you had good sense,' he told me," says Ray. " 'I knew you'd run away from that wildfire if it got close.' "

Then Mae and her little brother breathlessly pelted Nathan with questions. Did anybody get hurt? Did they really stop the blaze? How much land did the fire burn?

Their father told them that the volunteers did not even try to put out the fire. Instead they encircled the flames, felled trees, cut brush around the perimeter, and finally isolated the fire. At the last, six or seven acres of rolling land were left burning and smoldering, and Nathan said nothing would be left but charred stumps and logs.

"Dad told me that maybe in my lifetime I'd see the valley the same as it was that morning, but never in his life."

The next day Nathan confessed his folly to the owners of the land, but they refused to blame him. They said the brush heaps should not have been left there so long. They surveyed the ravished meadow and decided they would bring mule teams to clear away the rubbish and charred logs. They would plant Indian corn, pumpkins, beans, and tomatoes in the ashen remains.

"What a crop they had, what taste that food had," Ray remembers. Potash residue from the fire and the virgin nutrients of the meadow rendered the land fertile and its harvest bountiful. The owners decided to hold on to the land, and for that and other reasons, Nathan's dream of one day living there was never to come about.

The Great Depression reduced demand for Nathan's birch oil, but he refused to give up hope, continuing to struggle against the same old forces that had always made life in his area of the mountains so difficult. The fact that the entire country was in an economic slump might well have been unknown to Nathan and his neighbors; they had been poor long before the depression came and would be poor long after it had passed. Their fortunes were influenced by unknown, unseen players, the powerful industrialists and financiers of the outside world who were exerting more and more control over the commerce and natural resources of the region. For all Nathan's striving and suffering, for all his enterprise and labor, he never seemed able to fill his overall pockets.

Mother Rena reared her brood to follow the Golden Rule. She read her Bible each night by an oil lamp, and she lived her days by the Word and by the preachings of the bishops. Though she was loving and compassionate in the ways of her Jesus, she thought children should grow up under Old Testament discipline; they should be punished when they did wrong. That was how she was brought up, and she was grateful for the kind of person she had become. She reared her children according to stern precepts, and Ray began to grow in the way Rena hoped he would. He wanted to avoid punishment, and although Rena was not yet with them at the Pickbritches shack, he nonetheless tried to behave in the way he thought she would approve.

"I was pretty good and civilized and was teached the Bible by my mama. Now my dad didn't teach me that way. But Mama was real humble and good. Religious. Lived of the teachings of God."

Three months after the valley fire, Ray's eighth birthday came. He was to return to Bethel, the "little old free school" nearby where Teacher Farthing and others taught in a small wooden structure. On that same spot today stands a larger school, a substantial granite building.

Above Bethel Church there was at that time a copse of young trees where a truant schoolboy might hide from the sight of teachers. It did not occur to Ray to roam that far, or to stay out of school, but there were boys in school who grew up without the biblical strictness Ray had so early known.

Already he was growing tall and strong, but he was peaceable, and brawling was not something he wanted to admit to his mother, ever. So when the "wild boys" of Pickbritches approached him before school one sunny morning, he tried to appease them without giving in to them. They asked him to stay out of school to play "fox and dogs" up in the pine saplings beyond Bethel Church. Ray declined.

"It'd be doing wrong. The teacher'd find out and whop us."

"But if you don't go with us, you'll tell."

"Naw, I swear I won't."

"Yeah, you will."

"Boys, that's your business. You go on, and I'm going to school."

"Oh, come on, so you won't tell."

"My business is to go to school. I promise you can trust me. I won't tell."

Then one of the boys said he thought Ray was truthful. "He won't tell. Let's trust him. I believe he's telling it honest."

Six boys were missing that morning, but in those days children were often absent because parents needed them on the farm, especially during the fall harvest season. Scant thought was given the truant boys until noon recess rolled around. That was when Teacher Farthing sensed something amiss.

The game of fox and dogs had been played in Pickbritches long before Ray was born. Typically, two or three boys would be foxes; the others would be dogs. The fox would find a tree, usually a sapling that bent just to the right tilt under a boy's weight. The one playing fox would climb up and out on such a hidden sapling. The others would search the woods; they would sniff, bark, and howl just as fox-hunting dogs might. Once they discovered their quarry, they would climb up after the fox, who might jump from tree to tree to avoid his pursuers. If he was trapped in a tree, he would go out as far as he could before turning to fight.

"Odd gosh, some of them would climb them sloping trees like a red fox does, and when the 'dogs' came jumping out from the bushes, the 'fox' would fling over into another tree, or hit the ground and climb another one. They'd ride a little tree down to the ground, and if you caught one, he'd go at you like a cornered fox would. He'd go, 'agg, ha-a-a-ha, r-r-r-r' and the dogs would go to barking and howling. The fox would bite, scratch, kick. Put your eye out. Kill you. Gah, just like a fox. A fox will eat you up if you corner it. It'll gnash at you and bite you. Boys that played the game would do that, too, just like a fox. It was a rough game. When I got older I'd play the game, but I'd never put my hands on a fox."

When the fox was caught, the game would be over. Then new foxes would volunteer from the playing group.

Teacher Farthing heard the sounds of dogs, and he asked the other male teachers to go with him to the woods. Soon they were bringing back both foxes and dogs.

As the truants were marched past the other children, the largest of them yelled at Ray the timeless schoolyard threat: "We gonna git you!"

After class, Ray ran hard toward his shanty home, but the older Pickbritches boys overtook him. His diplomacy was useless now, and his reluctance to fight did not keep him from taking a thrashing.

"They liked to have killed me, to beat me to death."

As they pummeled and shoved him about, Ray kept talking:

"Gah, no! Don't beat me up. I swear I didn't tell. You'uns was a-barking, got carried away and forgot how close to the school you was. If you'd remembered where you's at, you'd have made it. But you got carried away. I never told on you'uns to the teachers. Never whispered a word or nothing."

One day Nathan hitched Zeb and Nick to the sled and drove back to Old Mountain Road to gather up his family's belongings. They would all move to be near Nathan's distillery, because there were economies in being together.

The Hickses moved into a house at nearby Beaverdam. Although they could bring but little food from a paltry harvest at the old homestead, they would still live a mite better than before. Nathan bought a nine-hundred-pound horse named Colonel; on Sundays he would hitch the animal to a buggy and drive Rena to see their families. One Sunday Rena took sick, and it was Ray who went along on the visit to his grandparents. Near Bethel Church, Nathan tightened the reins to control the buggy's speed, but Colonel's temperament took over, his gait quickened, and the buggy lurched forward. Strong Nathan stood up and again pulled the reins, but Colonel moved even faster; finally, Nathan yanked so hard that he drew the horse's rump hard against the dashboard. The buggy slowed to a manageable speed, but its front rubbed hard against Colonel's hide. As the conveyance bounced and Ray held on with both hands, hair flew from the horse's rump.

"Atter then, every time I'd speak of that time—when the horse's hair flew in my mouth—Dad would get tickled. When he was not feeling good, all I had to do was say, 'Yiah, hair flew in my mouth.' It'd always make him laugh."

High-spirited Colonel became known by nearly everyone in Bethel and Beaverdam. Once when Ray's oldest brother, Lewis, drove the sled behind Colonel, he brought the rig to a stop at Teacher Farthing's woodshed. Lewis wrapped the reins around a standard on the sled and hopped off. The horse, sensing he was not tethered, quickly broke for freedom.

The woodshed was close by the road and Colonel circled it, picking up speed as the sled bumped violently behind. Neighbors in the fields saw the flying rig coming; they knew it belonged to the Hickses, and they broke away from their work to surround Colonel. In the excitement, though, they did not remember that there was a path around the teacher's woodshed, and Colonel spotted the open driveway and headed for it. The sled caught against the woodshed, bringing it down. In a rising frenzy, the horse galloped off toward Beaverdam. The Hicks house, which had a short porch on the kitchen side, stood apart from the farm buildings there. When Nathan, who was working at the still, saw Colonel coming, he flung himself in pursuit; his sons, including young Ray, also joined in the chase.

"By the time we got to the house, our tongues were hanging out and we's all puffing wind," says Ray. "By then the horse was circling the house, and Mama came running out a-screaming. That didn't help any, and Colonel ran around the house with the sled knocking over the washpot and tearing up the gyarden. Made three circles around the house with Mama still a-screaming. The last time around, the sled caught on and tore off the porch.

"Odd gosh, what a mess. When the porch went the tin roof came down and made a noise you could hear all the way to Bethel. And Mama was crying and yelling: 'God, we've got it now. The house was ready to fall in already, and now it *will* fall.'

"Well, Colonel didn't want no more of Mama's screaming, so he took off up the mountain where he'd been pasturing. He knowed the pasture, you know, and when Dad went and found Colonel up there, the horse's hocks was nearly beat off his legs.

"Horses go crazy when they run away."

Ray's eldest sister Bessie had begun seeing the timorous Frank Proffitt, a young farmer who lived up Pickbritches Creek in the house of his parents, the Wiley Proffitts. Now that the Hickses had settled in at Beaverdam, Frank called often, bringing his guitar and singing old ballads, along with songs he "made up" about the depression.

On a day when Frank was to come over, Bessie typically would prepare a small treat for him. In the kitchen one afternoon she baked a cake for Frank, having hoarded small amounts of sugar and flour for such an extravagance.

Little brother Ray had become skilled with the hatchet. He had just cut a load of kindling and was bringing it to the kitchen when he espied the cake layers spread out on the table. Bessie had gone for a moment to tidy the parlor when she heard someone open the back door. She knew Ray had not eaten that day, and with him the cake layers might not be safe.

"If that's you, Ray, don't touch my cake layers," she shouted. But she was too late. As she rushed into the kitchen, Ray grabbed a piece of the cake and bolted out the back door. With Bessie screaming and in chase, Ray jumped from the porch still holding a cake layer. In disgust Bessie kicked an empty slop pail in the direction of her brother. Ray laughed as he ran, knowing Bessie's intent was only to make noise and chase him from the kitchen, but the top edge of the bucket nicked his ankle.

In a few days the small cut had begun to heal, and Ray regarded it as any other scratch a country boy might have. But later it became "scabbed over," and the injury began to bother him.

"I couldn't tetch it, couldn't put my foot on the ground. When I'd go to get wood I'd hop on one leg."

Even major injuries were normally treated at home. At most a "doctor"—schooled only in medical lore and traveling around on a horse with a few supplies in a saddlebag—might come. For scratches and bruises, it was unheard of to seek outside help. Home remedies—poultices of fatback, herbs, strong teas, or chewed tobacco wads—were used. Ray's festering wound, even his hopping

Hard Times on Pickbritches Creek

about, was not yet a concern. So he did his chores and continued going to school. Finally, though, his mother became worried and talked to Nathan.

"Better take Ray over yander to see Granny Williams. His sore's not getting better."

Granny Williams lived across the state line, and her first husband had been a "doctor" who rode through the mountains with herbal remedies in his bag. Now Granny had her own practice. Besides tending to the sick and injured, she helped in the "bairning" of babies anywhere she could travel within the region.

Nathan decided to take Ray to see Granny Williams. He put the boy on Colonel and led the way across a primitive road and through canyons and gullies. Ray remembers that his father grumbled along the way: "What trouble. And me and the burdens I've got already. What a worry a slop bucket can make."

After the woman looked at the wound, she told Nathan that he should have brought the boy to her sooner. Pointing to a place high on the Ray's thigh, she told the father that his son might lose the leg.

Ray gasped. He remembered horror stories of amputations. He knew that in the backwoods a handsaw might be used to cut off a badly mangled or infected limb. He had heard his father's cousin tell how only whiskey was given to cut the pain. He thought of his great-grandmother Rebecca, who as a little girl lost an arm in a sugar mill, and he remembered the man in Banner Elk who sawed off his own leg. That man later wore a homemade wooden leg; a blacksmith made a steel ring to place between the man's stump and peg.

"Granny Williams told Dad, said, 'I'm going to put on a poultice of whole wheat. You tell Rena, tell her to change it twice a day; bathe it and put on a poultice of whole wheat flour. Just like I did. Do that twice a day.'"

In the two weeks that followed, Ray thought often about the peg-legged man, the great-grandmother with one arm, the stories of others whose amputations had been performed with a carpenter's saw on a kitchen table.

Rena faithfully changed the poultices and washed Ray's wound. Bessie, who blamed herself, helped tend her brother. In deference to his healing leg, he hopped about less and rested often; in two weeks he was walking well. He would always remember the flour remedy.

"That's whole wheat, not bleached," he admonished friends. "That flour probably saved my life."

Soon after, Bessie Hicks and Frank Proffitt decided to marry. Because elop-

Hard Times on Pickbritches Creek

ing was a fashion, a farcical act in the neighboring settlements, a friend in Beaverdam offered to take Frank and Bessie across the Tennessee border to be married. He cranked up his old automobile and drove the young lovers over to Mountain City, where a magistrate performed the ceremony. They set up housekeeping in Pickbritches Valley, within sight of the dwelling of Frank's parents.

Nathan's distillery was lovingly crafted with copper fittings. Birch oil was made by a process similar to the making of whiskey. Vapor from the boiling birch mash would funnel through a pipe, where it was exposed to lower air temperature. Then, drop by drop, the steam liquefied and dripped into a can beneath a small shaved twig at the mouth of the pipe. The oil was so potent that a single pure drop would burn one's tongue. As the reddish, translucent liquid filled the can, the distillate sank to the bottom and the "backings" floated to the top. A half-gallon of birch oil weighed a pound, and that amount would bring three dollars from the Tennessee broker.

Nathan was not alone in distilling oil, but he produced more than anyone else around. In time he discovered that by running the backings through the still a second time he could increase his total output by one-fourth.

Today birch wood is processed for building uses; synthetic flavorings have taken the place of distilled birch oil. But in the twenties and thirties, Nathan manufactured both birch oil and wintergreen from the same distillery. By the standards of the impoverished people around him, he was a cut above the rest. He worked hard and his future seemed secure.

Then disaster struck.

The regular time came for the Tennessee distributor to pick up the birch oil, but the day passed with no sign of him, then another week. Finally Nathan learned there would be no more pickups. Buyers had discovered that the traveling jobber was diluting the oils he bought. Now they would buy elsewhere, and no other distributor came to collect birch oil again in the North Carolina mountains.

So in 1932 the Hickses gathered up their pots, pans, bedding, chairs, and eating utensils. They packed them on their sled and into a 1923 Model-T and wended their way back to Old Mountain Road, the "rough grade," the homeplace that had always sustained them, however poorly.

They set about to clean up the house, because it had been occupied by two families of renters who treated it badly. The last couple had distilled whiskey in the kitchen; smoke from the boiler had been vented through the chimney so that no revenue agent could detect the liquor making by sight.

Once when Ray was twelve, he and sister Mae made the pathless trek from Old Mountain Road to Beaverdam. On their backs, they carried clothes and food — gifts from Rena to Bessie and Frank. Ray and his sister spent the night there, but the young Proffitts "was seeing it hard," Ray recalls, and "they didn't have nothing to eat hardly." So the next morning the visitors set out for home, as Ray remembers it:

A long, hard journey,
a-climbing that mountain
down yander from the river;
it's straight up,
had to hit your knees
to walk.

And I was so hungry
and I saw rutabagas
set out in the corn,
or next to it there.
And my sister said,
"Ray, you'd better not . . ."
I said, "Odd gosh,
I'm going to get me
one to eat.
I'm so weak and hungry."

And we got on up
on the crossing gap
and he'd met me there
and made me eat it
in front of him.
Said, "Now son, eat it."

Hard Times on Pickbritches Creek

Said, "You took it
and never asked for it."
Said, "Don't you go back
through that nigh-cut no more."

I swear I didn't think
I was that much wrong
to eat one rutabaga.

Now it reads in the Bible
to get you something to eat
if you're out on a journey.
It's in the Holy Bible
where I've read it.
Been teached by the preachers.

Says if you're out
and take just what you hold
in your hand but not take
a sickle or not a vessel
to the vineyard.
That's meaning getting
too much.
And you's hungry,
to get what you c'n hold
in your hand.
If you're in the vineyards,
get two twigs of grapes.
Two twigs.
One in each hand.

They ain't no wrong with God
if you's out in a journey
and you's stranded.
Two twigs of grapes,
God wouldn't say nothing to you.

Hard Times on Pickbritches Creek

The man made me eat it
in front of him.
Said, "Make it taste, chew it."

Said, "Don't never come
through this nigh-cut no more."

My sister told me,
Said, "Starve it out, Ray."
But when we got home
it wuddn't nothing to eat.
I seed Mama set and cry.

With his business gone, Nathan would start over where he had left off several years before. He would plant potatoes and corn and cabbages; he would earn cash only for absolute necessities—meaning no coffee, no white flour, no new clothes. The family would have to make do.

"And he told us young'uns," says Ray, "that we'd have to go up on the Beech to pull galax and cut haw. Do that besides our other work. Said we'd need legal for taxes and for shoes.

"Winter was a-coming."

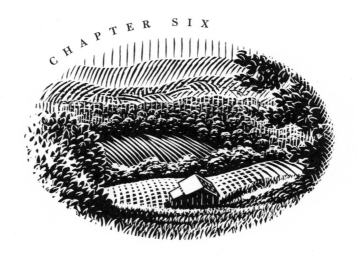

CHAPTER SIX

Little Boy of the Northwest Wind

Besides farming the land around his home, Nathan hired himself out as a field worker. When he was not working as a hired hand, he would dig ginseng or gather haw. He would go wherever there was money to be made.

The potato bug repeatedly wiped out most of his own crops, and he grew barely enough food to feed his family. Few storebought goods came into the home. When flour or lard ran low, Rena would send Ray to her parents' small store two miles away. Often the grandparents simply gave Ray the food he came for; other times they wrote down the purchase on a credit ticket.

Ray liked to visit the little store, which was next to his grandparents' house, down the hill from what is now known as the Old Andy Hicks Road.

"Yiah, they were named Hicks, too," says Ray. "Andrew Jackson and Suzy Ann Hicks. See, there was a lot of people out here who didn't have ways to get around. So they married second cousins, even first cousins. You won't find many different names in these parts: Wards, Hickses, Presnells, names like that; you'll see them on mailboxes. Everybody's kin to everybody else."

At the store, Andy and Suzy Ann sold staples and a few luxuries like licorice candy. They would buy and trade goods for herbs and roots, dry or green; if green, they would cure them in a cellar beneath the store and later take them to

Boone to sell. They also raised beans and potatoes, and Ray marveled that his grandparents' potato harvest was so much larger than his father's.

"Just, Ray ("Just," says Ray, was his grandfather's constant byword), if people would fight the potato bug, we'd get shed of it in these mountains."

It was from Andrew Jackson and Suzy Ann that Ray learned the qualities of patience and endurance that would stay with him all his life. Daily his grandparents went into the field and, plant by plant, killed the potato bugs by hand. Row by row they inspected their crop and crushed the eggs.

"Picked up field rocks, they did. Mashed them old bugs, or sometimes gathered them in a pan and poured scalding water over them," says Ray. "The bugs would fly in of the spring and lay eggs. They'd raise fast, and it ain't long before they've got a army a-going, just like a honey bee. They's millions of them a-eating and a-going. Get one patch eat up and you'd meet them a-flying, a-hitting agin you."

Such perseverance was common to Andy and Suzy Ann. It was from them more than anyone else that Ray learned to deal with adversity. Stoicism and constancy came to be part of his character.

In their first summer back at the big house, the Hickses missed Ray's sister Bessie. His mother, Rena, frequently with child, sorely felt the absence of her eldest daughter. She would call upon young Ray because he was dependable, but his usefulness was tempered by his young age.

Ordinarily Ray and the other children were given a pair of new shoes once a year. By spring their footwear was frazzled and useless, and during the summer they went unshod. This year Nathan could not be sure that he would have money for shoes. Meanwhile Ray watched his step; he tried to avoid stumped toes and bruises in order to protect his battered feet.

"I asked Mama what we'd do when winter comes. How can we go to school barefooted? She told me, she said, 'Somehow, Ray, the Lord provides.'"

So Ray took a deeper interest in the crops. He knew that a good yield of potatoes meant that one day he and his father would hike over the Beech and down to Heaton's Store; there he would be fitted in a pair of Red Goose shoes. But Nathan and Rena too often looked out over their acres and spoke of a bad harvest.

When Ray and his father started out on the eight-mile walk to Bessie's house one Sunday morning, Ray's feet were pocked with sores from his shoeless summer. He disliked the idea of such a long trek without shoes, but he did not complain; he wanted to see Bessie.

Ray walked ahead of his father, and a little more than halfway to Beaverdam, Nathan noticed the boy limping. Farther along he saw tiny spots of blood in Ray's tracks. At a roadside cornfield, Nathan stopped his son and looked at his feet. There were sores on the heels and cuts on the soles.

"Dad told me to wait," Ray recalls. "Said, 'Sit down on this rock and I'll be back in a minute.'"

Then Nathan went into the cornfield where roasting ears had begun to tassel. He removed two ears, stripped them, and came back to Ray with the shuckings.

"He told me to hold up my feet. Said, 'Let me tie these shuckings on them.'"

He wrapped the husks around Ray's heels and fastened the other ends around the toes. Now shod on both feet with tough corn coverings, Ray walked the rest of the way to Beaverdam before the makeshift moccasins wore through.

Bessie bathed the boy's feet in warm salt water laced with herbs; late in the day her husband, Frank, borrowed a Model-T to take Ray and his father back to Old Mountain Road.

Looking back, Ray thinks the romantic notion of happy barefoot boys must have come from city people, not from those who walked the rocky mountainsides.

"My feet would get callused and horny. But that didn't keep them from getting cut and bruised. See, the worst part of developing calluses is that they make stone bruises quicker than if the skin wasn't so tough.

"When I was a-driving the cow from the mountain down to be milked, I had to run barefooted . . . run the cow across chestnut burrs that was thick in the woods. I learnt that if I'd run fast my weight wouldn't stay on a burr long enough to stick to my feet. So I picked up my feet fast. It got to where I could crack green burrs with my heel. But I didn't do that much. If it was a dry burr it could go into your foot and then fester."

Today, as an aging man, Ray shuffles his feet slowly. His towering frame is bent, and he limps in favor of the same foot that always seemed to be in pain when he was a shoeless boy.

"It bothered me so, going down yander to the gristmill and to the post office. It was an awful steep path. I'd go down the banks with corn or buckwheat on my back, going to the gristmill to get it ground. And off of a steep place, little rocks would roll under my feet and my toes would scoot back under . . . tear the nails off and leave them hanging. Finally one toe slid back and got broke. It didn't grow back right, and so I had to start wearing a bigger shoe on that foot. Broke it at the joint and throwed it out of place. My toes is yet crooked."

It was while working in the cornfield that Ray became acquainted with the "facts of life." "The old people was teached to keep stuff hid from the kids, especially young kids," said Ray.

When the ten-year-old boy found a large hole on the hillside where a tree's decaying stump once stood, he asked grandfather Benjamin if a groundhog had made the hole.

Benjamin told him that a groundhog usually did not dig in an open meadow, that it burrowed under big rocks and tree stumps. " 'What you see there, Ray,' Grandpa told me, 'is where a cow dug out a calf.' "

Another time, when he asked his mother where he came from, Rena told him he was sent down from heaven in a feather ticking.

Then one summer day when Ray, a younger brother, and his father were hoeing corn, he heard their brindled milk cow on the hill above them.

Moo, she bellowed, suddenly kicking.

In the next instant Ray and his brother were stupefied by what they saw.

"All of a sudden a little cow came out of Old Brin and rolled down the hill. Not hurt. But Old Brin started atter the tumbling baby a-saying moo, moo, moo.

"Dad looked up and saw it and said, 'Damn.' Said, 'Old Brin's played hell; she's let it out. Guess you had to learn sometime.'

"The little calf just came out of Old Brin. Floop. And it hit the ground and rolled off that steep bank below the cliff. Nearly rolled into the little old road. And Brin was a-running atter it. She was a-mooing and going m-m-m, m-m-m. And trying to lick it, you know, to dry it off.

"And I knowed then. They couldn't fool me about groundhog holes and feather ticking no more."

Although the crops that year were poor, Nathan and Rena did manage to scrape together money for their children's shoes. September came, and Ray walked to and from Cool Springs School, more than three miles each way. If the weather was too severe, he would stay home.

Little Boy of the Northwest Wind

Early in the school year he would save whatever scrap paper he found because he did not have a tablet. Like many other mountain children, he had no money to buy writing paper. But the teachers understood. They too were mountain people; they shared the insight of poverty and at times gave their students prizes bought with their own money. Early that year Ray "beat" in spelling and arithmetic. His reward was a penny pencil and a writing tablet.

Scholarship, though, was not enough to spare him from beatings. In the way of their ancestors, mountain children frequently acted out disputes based on clan or family differences. Ray was a Hicks, and there was only one other Hicks pupil in school. The two children were often taunted and made the butt of jokes because they were among the poorest of them all.

Though he was tall and wiry, Ray was not feared by others. They knew that in deference to his pietistic mother he would not fight. Also, he was liked by his teacher and therefore became a playground target; he paid for his differences at the hands of tough gangs who followed him after school. They jeered and taunted, but the gangling boy ignored their insults.

Ray had won the writing tablet, but soon the paper would be gone. Knowing that there would be no money from the family to replace it, he would find a way himself. The rampant blight had not yet wiped out chestnuts in the Beech Mountain forests, and Ray—who had picked nuts since he was six—gathered the chestnuts and kept them in a box; when he had collected a peck, he'd take them to Mast's Store and sell them. Thus he was able to keep himself in tablets and penny pencils through the rest of the school year.

In the schoolroom, students sat at double-seated desks with scrolled cast-iron legs—boys together, girls together. Each desk had a drawer for books and a hole for an inkpot that was never filled. Up front, above the blackboard, was a picture of George Washington, paid for by students and teachers who sold packages of vegetable seeds. A potbellied stove warmed the room unevenly as the students did their lessons under the guidance of teachers who were well known in the community. The parents considered one instructor to be too rough and profane, but Ray thought him the best teacher and most generous person he knew.

On the day school closed for Christmas, this teacher brought bags of peanuts and candy he had purchased out of his own pocket. He passed down the aisles distributing the treats, and he heaped more upon Ray's desk than he did the others.

"Gah, you've given me too much," Ray protested.

The teacher bent down and spoke into Ray's ear: "He whispered," says Ray. "Told me, 'When I give something I want it to be enough to do some damn good.'"

The teacher's gift was the most Ray would get for Christmas. At home there would be an orange on Christmas morning, but, as the children well expected, nothing more.

In January Ray's feet so often became cold that he lost his toenails.

"Mama told me that I'd just have to stay home on days when it got so cold. Said, 'We need you here in the house anyways.'"

So on the wintriest days he did not walk to school, and he lost much of the luster of his scholarship. But he did not want to be truant, and there would be days when he walked the three miles without wool stockings under his battered shoes.

Around noon one day in early March, the children saw through the school windows that heavy snow had begun to fall. It was no surprise, because the mountains' heaviest snows come in late winter and early spring. By two o'clock it was apparent that a blizzard had set in, and the principal cut short the school day. For Ray and some others who lived far distant, the dismissal came late.

The boy left his books in his desk and began walking with a friend who soon reached home. From Devil's Highway onward, Ray trudged alone through mounting drifts. He stuffed his pants into his stockings and slogged past the old cheese barn and the church. He thought of the advice grandfather Benjamin had given him on another snowy day.

"If I hadn't done what he told me," says Ray, "I wouldn't have survived the storm."

The large, soft flakes of the morning now turned into small, driving, icy crystals, so dense the boy found it difficult to see the road.

"My eyes sleeted up with that throwing snow, and I had to keep stopping to wipe them so I could see."

He knew he was now less than two miles from the home of grandparents Andrew Jackson and Suzy Ann. But he knew that in such a blizzard it would take until nightfall to reach them.

"My clothes was no good and the wind would blow through them and just take my breath. I'd just dive my head in a snow drift till I could breathe. Just like Grandpa Benjamin told me. After ducking down to catch my breath I'd come

Little Boy of the Northwest Wind

back up, and the wind would cut through me again. Gah, the wind in this country's sharp and blowing."

The boy could now see no more than six feet in front of him, but he knew from the lay of the land that he was nearing the home of grandparents Andy and Suzy Ann. From their house on a clear day, Ray could see Elk Knob, Rich Mountain, Snake Mountain, and the blue-gray peaks that faded off into Tennessee and the Virginias. Today he could not detect even the fenceposts near the road; for moments that seemed like hours he became entangled in barbed wire.

Covered with snow and shivering from the wind and cold—his lungs seared by the frigid winds—the boy labored through new drifts to the door. Andrew Jackson and Suzy Ann gave him "coffee" made of toasted bread crumbs; they dried him with rags, placed quilts around him, and seated him near the large mudrock fireplace.

"Suzy Ann told me to stay the night," said Ray. "Told me my Mama wouldn't worry. Said, 'She'll know, just like we did, that you had the good sense to stop off here.'"

But Ray still thought of his mother. He wondered if Nathan, in a fit of "the miseries," had stayed away from home today. If so, the woodpile would be low, and the boy knew there was little food.

When Ray awoke the next morning, snow had drifted so high that only in a few places could he see the hog fences. After breakfast, wearing woolens his grandparents lent him, Ray set out on the final leg home. When he arrived, he could tell that neither mother nor children had ventured out from the dwelling. A gelid, white blanket had drifted above the delft knob at the front entry; the door obviously had not been opened since the storm began.

Ray kicked snow back across the porch into the entry yard; still, as he entered, it spilled into the icy sitting room. There was no fire and no wood in the box. The boy wandered through the quiet house and found his younger brothers and sisters fully clothed and in their beds. Older brother Lewis was away. Ray knocked on the front bedroom door and his mother answered feebly. He knew for certain now: besides no firewood, there was no food.

"Dad was gone," said Ray. "He'd give up. He got broke up in his nerves. We didn't know where he was. Lewis, too, was out; got caught out in the blizzard at a friend's place the day before. And me, just a ten-year-old boy, here alone with Mama and the kids. I knew I'd have to help take care of them."

Not expecting such a blizzard, Rena had depleted the available stack of

Little Boy of the Northwest Wind

wood. Then the storm came and there was no wood nearby. The trees of the Hickses' own land had been cleared for pasture; in addition, a forest fire around their farm two autumns earlier had consumed the woods close to them. Except for the great ash tree just off the porch—too large to chop down in the wintry storm—there was no fuel nearby. The nearest firewood lay under snow, high on Beech Mountain. Without a wheelbarrow, the only way to bring wood back would be armload by strenuous armload. There was no longer even a sled on which the wood could be hauled.

Ray searched for a kitchen match. He would go out again, perhaps take the next oldest child, and climb the mountain to dig out armfuls of deadwood from the forest floor. He would come back and light the driest and smallest twigs to create a bed of coals. Then the larger and wetter pieces would burn. To keep a blaze fueled through the day and night, he would need to make many trips up the mountain.

But the search for a match turned up nothing. When he talked with his mother, he found that she had tried two days before to buy matches and food at a little store, but the owner could no longer extend credit to the Hicks family.

Yet firewood would be of no use if it could not be ignited. So Ray's thoughts turned to making fire without a match, a primitive skill Benjamin had taught him. He would need a "quilt mat" of spunk, called "dodie wood" in the mountains, and flint rocks for catching the sparks.

He searched for dodie wood: "The best comes from an old sugar tree—rotted dodie wood, where the tree's hollowed out and the wood inside is fine as wheat flour; then you can lay that on your hearth to make a mat that will catch fire when you make a spark.

"Now just any kind of rock won't make that blaze. The striking rock has to be flint, like the Indians used; the other rock has to be a good flat one. Strike the sharp flint on the other'n and it'll run a blaze off the rocks *that* long." He measures a couple of inches with thumb and forefinger. "Just flick them together and there'll be a blaze of fire."

Finally the boy found a tobacco tin filled with dodie wood, but there were no matches, no flint rocks, no firewood; he realized that without the resourceful Nathan the family was unprepared for such an emergency.

A new wind arose, and through the bare windows Ray could see snow whirling like tiny swifts. Thin sheets of wind knifed through the cracks of the house, and Ray thought of tramping down to the house of Benjamin and Julie; he

Little Boy of the Northwest Wind

could see wisps of smoke blowing from their chimney a half-mile away. He could "borrow fire" and bring it home through the deep drifts. But he would need many loads of wood, too.

"No," he told himself, "Grandpa Benjamin is too old to help; I wouldn't even ask him; he might have a heart attack helping me tote wood over here."

Then Ray worried that the fine, spitting flakes might give way to a snowless cold, that frigid winds would build out of the northeast mountains, encrusting the snow with ice; and the children might freeze in their beds.

"Odd gosh, I thought. Where could Dad be?" Ray sat down and looked around; the house was dark and sad. The icy glow from outdoors winnowed through the glass panes but only faintly lightened the somberness. Ray went again to the window and was heartened to see specks of silver still swirling. More snow, he thought, was better than ice crusting over the white surface. His eyes cast slowly about the lifeless room, but it was a strain to call up past images of so much warmth and vitality: ancient stories spun, banjos and dulcimers played, his family singing, himself doing the buck dance. How mean it would be if this place that had known so much life would see his early death. His mind raced over ways he could save the family from freezing and starving, but still the dark thoughts remained.

Then he heard a noise.

Up the hill there was movement. Beyond the crest and barely visible against a brilliant background, there seemed to be two white horses and possibly a sled; but they appeared to be moving away from the house toward Andy Hicks Road. Ray rushed to open the door, to call to the driver; then he saw a figure working its way downhill toward the ash tree.

Someone had brought Lewis home.

The old house suddenly came to life, and Ray hurried from the porch to grab his brother.

" 'Gah, Lewis,' I said. 'We've had it. I come home and find Mama and the kids with no wood and no vittles. Dad ain't here and I don't know what to do.' "

Lewis beat the snow from his feet and told Ray they would have to make haste. "He said he had a lighter and all we needed was to scrounge some wood."

The brothers talked excitedly. They decided to go outside and dig into the drifts; they pulled several rails out of the hog fence and dragged them into the parlor. There they cut up the lengths of firewood with a hatchet, stripping one length into thin pieces for kindling.

They laid a fire by sprinkling the dodie wood on the kindling strips. Soon the blaze caught and they added lengths of fence railing.

"The kids and Mama came out of their beds and we gathered around the old fireplace right there. Got warm from wood off the hog fence. They forgot how hungry they was."

Ray missed school often that winter. There were days of unendurable cold and entire weeks when his mother needed the boy at home. Sister Bessie, living too far away to help, remembers that her mother was "sickly" and often needed assistance.

"Never did know what was wrong with her, but she would get real sick . . . stayed in bed most of the time."

In those days, old methods of caring for the ill prevailed. When a woman had children—and most women had many—she stayed in bed for weeks before and after the baby came. Bessie herself broke away from the pattern when her little ones came along, but she remembers the old ways with distaste.

"When they had young'uns back then, the mother stayed in bed because they didn't want her to get out and catch some other disease. The mother had to sleep in the same bed for six weeks after the baby was born, and the sheets couldn't be changed. They'd put a cap on the baby and wouldn't let you change the cap until the baby was two or three months old. When the cap was taken off, the little head would be dirty and covered with dandruff."

During their confinements, mothers were waited on by family and neighbors. Bessie once watched Nathan try to make biscuits: "Just pure salt."

Without Bessie in the house, the job of caring for Rena fell to Ray, who was not the oldest at home but the one upon whom Rena could most rely.

"Mama, why do you holler for me all the time?" Ray asked. "And she told me I was the only one with a feeling to help her."

Staying home from school took its toll. From his beginning as a bright, promising student, he fell behind. Absences of two and three days at a time, often more, were a trial for both Ray and his teacher, and the boy became confused and discouraged. Soon nearly every pupil in his class moved ahead of him. Rena would say tearfully: "I'd like to keep you in school all the time, but if you don't help work here, we'll all die."

It was during this period that mental depression fitfully overtook Nathan. Too often he dwelled on his failures, and at these times he ranged far from the home-place, leaving his family perplexed and in want. To Ray and his mother, it was a winter of dread:

We was snowed up
and Dad gone,
we didn't know where,
he'd got to drinking.

Mama said he treated her good
till he got thirty years old.
Then he took to drinking liquor,
that old mountain liquor.

He was gone
and we was snowed up here
with a big snow on,
and not a bite in the house.
She was a-crying
and I'd [say] "Mama, hang on,
hang on.
God wants us to live."

With Nathan away so often, Ray was drawn to his mother's gentle and contemplative ways. He had learned from school that people from other places were strangely different from the folk of the quiet, beautiful valleys he knew. His own people were harder up, they clung to old ways, and they were suspicious and perhaps even afraid of the outside world.

So one day followed another on Old Mountain Road, and life was much the same. The stories recounted by Ray's elders told him that times had never been much different. No matter how hard they worked, the deck was always stacked. Someone else held the face cards, while the Hickses and their kin and neighbors held the twos and threes.

As the boy hoed potatoes and gathered wood, he thought of the stories told to him by the fires of a mountain winter. He was not aware that these same tales might have been recited to children by peat fires in another country in another time. He was driven by the sense, however, that he was divinely appointed to preserve the stories, to perpetuate the ways of his beloved people. He keenly felt the challenge of passing along the old ways to new generations. As he worked in the fields he told over to himself ballads and tales that might date back hundreds of years—kept alive by pioneers who came to a new country and continued the old traditions even as they created new adventures, new songs, new stories. In his repertory, Ray embraced the cultures of many ages.

Hard as Ray worked in the forests, he often rested and observed his surroundings.

"The animals talking to one another; little mice working with you; chipmunks, gray squirrels, all eating up the chestnuts, and the birds pecking them. Grouse looking for their food on the rough ground. Yiah, grouse. The old people thought they was pheasants, but that's a ring-necked; our'n come from the rough grouse. And the grouse swallowed the chestnuts and acorns.

"People say birds and little animals don't talk to each other. But they do. We just don't know their language.

"One time down yander I went to where the grouse would eat possum grapes, that wild possum grape that would grow in the valleys of the woods and forests. They would eat them atter it frosted. And green briar berries. I was down in there a-pulling galax and saw where they's feasting on them grapes. They'd be three or four of them on the ground pecking at the grapes and they'd be facing each other like a family a-setting around the table. One would stop eating and look around like it was talking to the others at the dinner table.

"And then the boomer. Some call it a red squirrel; but in the mountains it's always called a boomer . . . halfway between a chipmunk and a gray squirrel. Gah, it'll eat your house up.

"So, I was out where all that hemlock timber was over on the Beech, and I saw a little boomer come to eat the hemlock's new buds. I went and set on an old hemlock stump. Hid myself a little. And that boomer knowed. It recognized; smelt a human. It went chi, chi, chi, telling the others that there was somebody there. You could tell by the sound of its talk.

"I had my gun, but I said, 'I ain't going to shoot that little animal.' Now some people would shoot it right away because a boomer might knock them out of shooting a grouse. Shoot it just as quick as it would come out, get it out of the way. Shoot it quick. Kill it. See, they's knocking the hunter out of his game.

"Then a grouse come through and the boomer run off. But I just set up on my stump till the grouse left. I knew the little boomer would come running atter that, come back to the hemlock buds.

"Well, I was setting still on the stump and that little boomer come running back toward the hemlocks. It didn't even notice that I wasn't part of the stump and it just ran right up the stump, up my back, and stopped on my right shoulder. Thought I was part of the stump. It set there awhile, and I said, 'Gah, it might bite me on the neck.' I thought I might catch it around the neck with my left hand so I could tell people I'd caught a boomer setting on my shoulder. But when I moved a little it jumped thirty feet up. It went chi, chi, chi. It called to the others and said, 'You'uns better beware.' Said, 'I was setting on his shoulder and come in one of being caught.' "

Ray often says of the Jack Tales: "Just listen. They's a lot that's not true, but a lot that is."

The truth is interwoven with the myth. The stories handed down in the coves of Beech, Laurel, and Spice Creeks were fluid and timeless, often told with rhetorical brilliance. Tales normally began with hunger, despair, and ignorance but ended in feasts, happiness, and triumph; in this, they reflected the condition and dreams of humble people through the centuries. The stories often changed subtly to conform to changing norms. In the tales Benjamin and Julie related to Ray, the dwarf's hovel of the past might become a tinsmith's cottage and finally a mountain man's cabin; a guinea might become a quarter; a dragon might now be a mountain lion.

When Ray, in his lyrical eloquence, narrates the story, he knows that its value goes beyond a simple plot to speak truths born of rampant imaginations. It is no wonder that, after recounting the episode of the blizzard and his family's near death by freezing, he relaxes. Then he tells a story he calls "Jack and the Northwest Wind."

Now, Jack and his mama was together in the old log cabin. The cabin he was raised in. But his brothers was married off and gone. His father was deceased

Little Boy of the Northwest Wind

. . . left him and the mama with just an old poleaxe. With that axe he tried to cut wood for the mudrock fireplace.

That wind, where they stayed at, that northwest wind . . . gah, hit would come through and just burn the house . . . like I've had it here . . . just burn the house. So Jack said, "Mama, I'm gonna go get you a bunch of wood and I'm gonna go till I find that hole and put my cap in it and stop the northwest wind from blowing." So cold of a wintertime where we live and others. Jack's mama said, "Well, if you can find that hole, that's be good."

So Jack got up and took off. Walked and walked. Passed log cabins fur apart from the other'ns. That's because people had to build where the mountain springs was at. They couldn't dig a well. They knowed nothing about getting no well water nor nothing. So he walked and finally came to a log cabin where a man was outside a-cutting wood with a poleaxe.

"Hello, son," the man said. "Why be on your way?" Jack said, "Man, that northwest wind has blowed so at home till I've decided to go hunt the hole where the wind's a-coming out at. Gonna put my hat in it. Gonna stop the hole up with my cap."

"Gosh, son," said the man.

And Jack said, "Me'n my mom ain't got nothing to eat much—no vittles, and we's about to starve, and hit so cold."

"Well," said the man. "Don't go stop up the hole. Just go back home. I'll give you a tablecloth that all you have to do is spread it out and say, 'Spread, spread, vittles, spread tablecloth full of vittles.'"

[As the yarn lengthens, Ray half rises from his chair; his arms wave; his eyes widen. He is living old experiences, elaborately disguised personal adventures. He has known cold, has known hunger. Such a story is best told by one who has lived it.]

And the man at the cabin said, "Now take the tablecloth and go back home. But don't stay at that little cabin you might have seen kind of hidden in the forest. Best that you don't even stop there. They's brothers there, ruggish boys, pretty rough." Said, "They're awful to want to take stuff off people. When they see the tablecloth, they'll say, 'What is that thing?'" Says, "They don't know what a tablecloth is probably." So, he said, "Don't stay all night there." Said, "They could take the tablecloth, put another'n in place of it. No, just you don't stay all night there. Leave."

And so Jack went on there, and he was a-feeling so big because he knew how to make that magic tablecloth work. So he passed that cabin where the rough boys was, him with the tablecloth under his arm, and them boys said, "Stranger boy, what have you got?" And Jack said, "I've got a tablecloth that the feller give me back yonder." And said, "I's going to stop up the northwest wind hole with my cap, put in that hole; but the feller give me the tablecloth if I'd just go back home. He told me to say, 'Spread, tablecloth, spread full of vittles.'"

"We don't believe no sich stuff as that," the mean boys said, "But, gah, we'd have to see you try it."

So Jack just spread the tablecloth down on the ground and said, "Spread, tablecloth, spread full of vittles." Them boys was hungry, and they looked and said, "Gosh, it did work." Said, "Let's eat." And they all ate full. And when it was all gone, Jack just rolled his table cloth back up and them boys said, "Go stay all night with us." Said, "What's yore name?"

Jack knowed not to stay, because the man told him, but he just figgered it'd be all right to stay anyway. And so he stayed. But while he was asleep that night, the boys and their daddy and mama stole his tablecloth and left one the same color as Jack's. One that was no good. Had no chantment in it.

Well, Jack got on home and said, "Mama, we don't have to worry about nothing to eat no more when we's hungry." Said, "I've got a tablecloth that will make all the vittles we need, every meal." And Jack put the cloth on the table and nothing come on. And, gah, he was hurt. He said, "I've seed it work, Mama, but it's no good now." Said, "I'm going back tomorrow and I ain't gonna listen to that man no more." So he went back the next day and come to the man and said:

"I'm a-going to stop that wind. The tablecloth worked for a while; then it quit."

"Did you stay with them boys, like I told you not to?" the man said.

"Yeah," said Jack.

"Well," said the man, "they've took it and put another'n in its place." Said, "They had one the same color. Fooled you up." Said, "Now here's a hen." Said, "Now you take this hen and go back. Hit lays golden eggs." Said, "Just put a bowl under it and say, 'Lay eggs, hen lay, come gold come.'" And said, "Hit'll lay that bowl full of golden eggs."

Little Boy of the Northwest Wind

So the man called on the hen and got the golden eggs—dropped one every five or ten minutes. And so Jack took it and went back, and he got to the cabin where the mean boys lived.

And they said, "What's that you got now, Jack?" And Jack said, "I've got a hen that lays golden eggs." The boys said, "Gah, we've got to see that tried, Jack." So Jack set the hen down and called on it, and every five minutes a golden egg would drop down, and the boys would grab it. "Gah," they said, "Hain't that something to see." Said, "You got to stay all night with us a-night." So Jack give up and went to bed.

"When Jack went off to sleep, they swapped another hen in his hen's place. Looked just like Jack's, couldn't hardly tell no difference.

Jack toted the hen home and showed his mama. He told the hen, "Lay hen, lay." But nary a egg come. And his mama says, "I told ye." And Jack said, "Well, I seed the hen do it before. Seed the man get the eggs from the hen, and seed it done before them boys. Now, it won't lay none." Said, "I'm going tomorrow to put my cap in that hole where the northwest wind comes from." Said, "That man's not stopping me this time."

So he got there to the man's cabin and told him what happened, that he was going on to dam up the northwest wind. And the man said, "Did you stop with them boys?" And Jack said, "Yeah, bedad, I stopped." And the man said, "Well, they got y'r hen like they got yore tablecloth." He said, "Here's a club, a playaway club. Just say, 'Playaway, playaway club.'" Said, "And the club'll do any beating, anything you want done." So he showed the club a block of wood and told it to split that wood open and put it on the porch. So the club did what he said and then it cut down a tree or two and the man stopped it. Said, "Now, see. That's what it does." And Jack took it and, boy, he's carrying it under his arm. And he's tickled.

He got on there and the boys, and gah, they said, "Now Jack, what ye got this time?" Jack said, "I've got a club that'll do any beating or anything I want to do." They said, "Gah, we'd like to see that tried. They's a big dead tree up yander on the ridge." And Jack said, "Playaway club, playaway." Said, "Go up yander and beat that tree down and put it on the wood pile and beat it up into sticks and rick it up on the porch. Then if they need a fire, knock it on the fire-place so the fire can burn it."

And hit went up there and knocked the dead tree down and knocked it into the woodpile, a-beating and a-knocking, and got it all worked up and put the

Little Boy of the Northwest Wind

wood on the porch. And the boys said, "Gah, Jack." Said, "Shorely you got to stay all night with us tonight." And so Jack give up again and went to stay the third time. He went off to sleep right beside the old mudrock fireplace, Jack did, because he was weared out.

And so, them boys' father come in late in the night, and they wanted to show him what the playaway club'd do. Didn't want to let Jack know it, and they just said, "Playaway club, playaway." Said, "Go out and knock some wood up." And it went out there, the club did, and got into a piece of wood, and the splinters was a-flying. Their dad's eyes popped out. They said, "Now bring it on the porch, and some of that in the house." And it knocked it in the house. And by that time, the racket and all, woke Jack up. It was getting down past midnight towards morning. And Jack heared it a-beating and he run out and said, "Playaway club, playaway." Said, "Beat the house down, if it takes it till they give me back my tablecloth and hen."

So the playaway club started beating the house, was a-beating the ceiling off the walls, and splinters was a-flying, and they all was a-running, them boys was. And Jack said, "Now get up on the roof." And the playaway club a-beating them boards and splinters a-flying. And them boys come with the tablecloth and the hen, a-begging Jack to stop the playaway club. Said, "We don't know what to say to stop it. Here's yore tablecloth and yore hen, Jack. Get that thing to stop." But Jack let it do a good beating. Said, "Let it beat a lot of the roof off." Then he said, "Quit, playaway club, quit, playaway. You done a-plenty."

And when it quit, Jack had his tablecloth, his hen, and his playaway club. He took them all home and showed his mama: of the vittles the tablecloth made, and they ate; of the golden eggs, his mama picking them up; and of the playaway club that Jack told to "Go yander and beat that dead tree down and bring some wood into the house." And the playaway club knocked down the tree, chopped it into firewood, and stacked it on the porch.

And Jack and his mama lived on easy, whatever time they lived after that.

"And that's the tale of the northwest wind," says the old storyteller. "I like to tell that'n whenever I can."

As Ray sometimes warns when he begins or ends a story: "It ain't true. But there's a lot that's true in it." Perhaps such tales recall dreams of "living easy" by the real little boy of the northwest wind.

Little Boy of the Northwest Wind

CHAPTER SEVEN

The Troubadours, the Tragedy

By 1938, the summer he turned sixteen, Ray had already grown past six feet. He had been the child upon whom his mother most depended, but now that the eldest son, Lewis, had moved away, he would also become the crutch of a father who wavered between flurries of industry and binges of despair.

As months passed, the boy learned to conserve his strength and stamina; he had seen Nathan continually expend his energies in enterprises that never seemed to pay off. Still, he could not understand why his father always blamed himself for failing to scale the walls of his economic prison.

Like cold molasses, cash had always oozed grudgingly into the settlement. The typical family under the Beech accepted privation and considered riches to be the lot only of kings and lords or the like. Yet Nathan drove himself beyond the capacity of his talent and knowledge; he harbored nameless ambitions and formless plans, sometimes to the point of obsession.

The Hicks children began to suffer from their father's passions; they did not eat as well as their mountain neighbors, and now there was no cow. Earlier, because of Rena's frequent illnesses, a baby had died soon after birth, and when Jack, the last of the Hicks children, was born in January 1938, he often did not have enough milk. When guests dropped in for dinner, as they not infrequently did in those days, the Hickses might serve only cornbread and water. At such times, it was common for Ray and the other children to eat nothing.

While people on the far side of the mountains took false hope from a peace pact signed in Munich that year, the Hickses and their neighbors neither knew nor cared about events taking place across the ocean. They rarely read newspapers and did not own a battery-powered radio. Even those who heard the news considered the world outside none of their affair. Dwellers in other lands might have their problems, but Beech Mountain people had their own; they dealt simply with failed crops and awesome need. Some neighbors left their families to join the WPA in Tennessee, and they considered the few dollars they earned as fortunes. But the government could not hire all the hill people who wanted jobs. The answer for some, as Ray Hicks remembers, was to leave their mountains and go to work in Detroit or Cleveland or Cincinnati. Many departed for the big cities; most of them never returned.

Men like Nathan, though, put their faith in their native skills, and few of his kind strayed from their own ridges and valleys, feeling unprepared for work beyond the mountains. Nathan himself hewed railroad ties from dead chestnut trees; he cut and sold tanbark, called "acid wood"; he made banjos and dulcimers and picked herbs and galax. Still, his family suffered and his self-esteem plummeted. To rally his spirits, sometimes in the evenings he would sit and strum his fretless banjo.

"Gah, Dad could make a banjo talk," says Ray, his intonation falling to a whisper. "His way of driving out his suffering, sometimes."

And Ray, whose great-uncle Roby Hicks (Stanley's father) had made a banjo for him, would often play too. Together, Nathan and Ray sang sad songs. It made them feel good to remind themselves of people who were more pained, even if they existed only in myth.

Then, out of the blue one day in the spring of 1939, a wonderful thing occurred: In a glorious twinkling of time, the inner muse that drove Nathan Hicks began to soar anew.

From New York a letter arrived. Frank Warner, a YMCA official who liked to sing folksongs, had seen a dulcimer owned by a college professor. The professor told Warner that he obtained the instrument from a man and his small son who performed one Saturday on a street in a North Carolina mountain town. Warner told the professor that he must own such an instrument; he obtained Nathan Hicks's address and wrote immediately.

Nathan welcomed the order and set about crafting a dulcimer. But glue, nails, and stain required money he did not have; nor could he afford the postage for shipping. So he wrote Frank Warner and was elated when a check came back to cover both the instrument and mailing expenses.

The making of that dulcimer set off a flow of happy events. Warner told his friends about Nathan, and this launched a spate of mail requests for dulcimers, one from the author and folklorist Carl Carmer. Warner, who with his wife Anne had begun corresponding with the Hickses, asked Nathan to make a banjo; he wrote that he, Anne, and their two young boys would drive from New York to pick up the instrument; they also would like to collect songs from the people Nathan knew around Beech Mountain. Meanwhile, Anne collected and sent donations of clothes. The Warners' entry into the lives of the Hickses, Proffitts, and Presnells began to change things. Over the next several years, people under the Beech looked at themselves and at the world beyond in a brighter way.

The regeneration began when Nathan made and sent the first dulcimer to Frank Warner. That purchase convinced Nathan that people outside Watauga might like to buy his homemade products. "Dad was the first around," Ray recalls, "to ship banjos and delcimores." Initially, Nathan asked only three dollars for an instrument, but Warner urged him to charge five.

In June the Warners loaded their car with clothes and food and drove down from New York. When they arrived at the house on Old Mountain Road, they were overwhelmed by the openhearted Hicks welcome, surprised by the stir their visit created.

In the afternoon, Frank Warner unpacked his guitar, and his wife prepared to write down lyrics as sung by the Hickses. Rena pulled down her cache of ballads from the cupboard; she drew from it yellowed envelopes and scrap paper upon which, since girlhood, she had scribbled the words to ancient songs. In Rena's collection, the Warners found treasures. It was at this point that the New York couple began in earnest to collect folksongs.

Soon Stanley's father, Roby, arrived. He had walked all the way from Spice Creek carrying his fretless banjo. Then came Ray's sister Bessie and her husband, Frank. On the way from Pickbritches Creek—eight miles distant on a dusty, rocky road—they took turns carrying their young son and Frank's guitar. Later Stanley's brother Linzy and cousin Vance Presnell dropped by—all dressed in Sunday clothes. They brought dulcimers, fiddles, banjos, and a guitar; they wanted to sing and play for the man who had ordered Nathan's home-made banjos and dulcimers, whose wife had sent packages from New York. They wanted mightily to please the guests from afar.

They gathered just off the front porch, under the shade of the spreading ash tree. Nathan placed a few straight chairs in the yard within hearing of the spring's trickle. He sat on the ground with his dulcimer, and throughout the gentle mountain afternoon they all played: "Bo Lamkin," "Hard Times on Beaverdam Road," "Going Up Cripple Creek," "Drunkard's Doom," "Wild Bill Jones."

At times the older troubadours laid down their instruments and listened to the ardent singing of Frank Proffitt. Anne Warner made particular note of the first tune young Proffitt sang; it was called "The Ballad of Tom Dooley."

Hang down your head Tom Dooley
Hang down your head and cry . . .

This song did not originate in the Old Country. Rather, it is the saga of young Tom Dula of neighboring Wilkes County, who was hanged for the killing of a former sweetheart.

The ballad had been handed down from the late 1800s, and one of Frank's first memories was of his father, Wiley, singing it one early morning. His grandmother, Adeline Pardue Proffitt, claimed that the version of the song she knew came from Tom Dula himself. Some say Dula played the song as he rode his coffin to the hanging, but Adeline vowed she heard Dula himself singing the ballad in his cell on the day he was hanged. Still others insisted that the ballad originated after Dula died. The name Dula was called Dooley in the mountains, just as Rosa became Rosie and Rena became Renie.

The ballad had spawned many variations in the seventy-five years before the mountain musicians sang it for the visiting Warners, but it was Frank Proffitt himself who added the lines:

Hadn't been for Grayson
I'd be now in Tennessee.

Twenty years later, the old song would be recorded and played around the world. But few people realize that its grand tour began beneath an ash tree that still stands just off Ray Hicks's porch on Old Mountain Road.

After Frank and Anne Warner went home, they remained in touch with Nathan and Rena and with Frank Proffitt. Letters flowed between New York City and the little post office at Rominger. In the city, Frank and Anne showed their dulcimer and banjo to illustrious guests. Upon the banjo that Nathan Hicks made, the Warners gathered the signatures of folk-music greats, including those of poet and author Carl Sandburg, singers Burl Ives and Pete Seeger, and world-renowned guitarist Andrés Segovia. The Warners told their friends about the dwellers "under the Beech": how proud and dignified they were; how deeply sensitive and intelligent, even in their destitution. Soon Nathan was mailing folk instruments to points throughout the country. At last, it seemed, he had found his place among the important people of the world beyond Beech Mountain. Rena, too, enjoyed a new prosperity when Anne Warner's New York friends began sending her orders for hooked rugs. She was bolstered by the attention and went about the house with renewed vigor.

The Warners' visit had created a kind of renaissance in the small community. Along the banks of Spice, Laurel, and Beech—streams that flowed down Beech Mountain into its shadowed coves—many local folk seemed to emerge from a dreary languor to revive their old enjoyment of music and dance.

Because Roby Hicks and his wife, Buena Vista (Buny), could play so many instruments, they quite naturally received music-loving friends at their cabin. Sons Stanley and Linzy and daughters Hattie and Rosie, all musicians, joined their parents to entertain their guests. But Linzy, a serious and pious young man, would politely leave when daring folk songs were played. His was a primitive mountain religion that did not tolerate flighty songs.

There still lingered in the region many customs that predated contemporary residents. Occasionally (although these were in eclipse) there were chivarees—rollicking serenades to celebrate weddings that dated back to England and Scotland. There were house raisings, barn raisings, molasses boils, and honey-tree robbings. Often, for no reason at all, some families would host singing and dancing in their barns or would clear their parlors of furniture to make a place for hearty soirees. For many months in the wake of the Warners' visit, these events reached fevered heights in the Watauga backcountry.

Roby and Buny began hosting jamborees every Saturday night. Sometimes the music makers would merely play and sing; other times they would provide lusty music for dances called by one of the guests.

"Buny didn't drink at all," Ray recalls, "but Roby was known to have a nip now and then. So I remember being there one night, and Roby stopped playing his banjo. He had cut his hand making dulcimers and he started rubbing it; he said to Arky, 'Arky, my old hand is hurting and hell-fired stiff and I can't pick.' And Arky said, 'Let's go out and get us a drink of water, Roby, maybe that'll help.' Well, they went out for a few minutes and come back in. Roby got the fiddle tuned up, got the banjo tuned up. Buny saw that Roby's hand didn't seem to be hurting, and she said, 'Roby, why didn't you bring me a little of that kind of water?'

"Now Arky had that good kind of water. Aged in a charcoal barrel for eleven years. It had songs in it. The other kind that most of them drunk had fourteen fights to the pint."

Roby and Buny encouraged their young to play, but seldom did any of them perform outside their Spice Creek sphere. When daughter Hattie was grown, she often danced when Buny played at schoolhouse concerts. They went to nearby counties in Tennessee, sometimes traveled to Asheville, and once were driven "somewhere down in Georgia" to perform.

Even in her nineties, living in a nursing home, Buny could still play her instruments and was once awarded a trophy by a nearby college. Son Stanley made dulcimers and banjos and played at "concerts" until his health failed.

The Warners came to Watauga again in 1941, but after that the rationing of gasoline during World War II prevented their return for many years. Memories of their visits faded, and many young mountain men were called into service in the war. Neighbors stowed away thoughts of a once-delightful diversion and returned to the grind of survival. Still, Rena Hicks and Anne Warner continued to exchange letters, and the New Yorkers were remembered in the settlement.

Although the first music-making frenzy waned, the mountain people were, as always, never far removed from their singing and dancing. They stashed their dulcimers, guitars, fiddles, banjos, and harmonicas under beds and behind doors, to be brought out again at the slightest suggestion. Music was a constant accessory of their austere existence, and little coaxing was needed for them to revive old songs and dances.

As they worked in the fields, they sang mournful songs. And on treks to Elk Park, Valle Crucis, or perhaps Cranberry, they might take along a harmonica, a banjo, and a jug of wine.

Ray likes to retell the story of one of these journeys. One summer morning his father Nathan, his grandfather Benjamin, and his uncle Samuel loaded Nathan's wagon with chestnut crossties. They would take these to the narrow-gauge railroad that served the Cranberry iron mines, and there Nathan would sell the crossties for twenty-five cents apiece. It would take his yoke of oxen most of the day to pull the load there, so the men counted on spending the night in the wagon. At such times, one of the men would pull a banjo from under the wagon seat and the group would sing by their campfire—their way of turning work into play.

After unloading the wagon, the three started for home, and when they reached a point near Skalley, off the slopes of Beech Mountain, they pulled the oxen off the road to rest for the night. Nathan played a few tunes on his banjo, and they all sang. Singing would help them forget their hunger; they had last eaten at dawn.

Yet as the singing wound down, they became ravenous for food. They could not find blackberries or blueberries growing along the road, but soon they spied a chicken pecking in the furrows of a nearby field. They crept stealthily from the wagon and approached the bird. Sensing danger, the fowl zigzagged quickly across the clearing, with the trio running after it. In a fever to catch their dinner, they did not realize that they had circled a patch of woods and reached the immediate yard of a farmhouse.

Out the door bounded a broad-shouldered farmer. The marauders froze in their tracks. Should they run or stay put and admit their mischief? Then, much to their relief, the farmer laughed. He did not rush toward them in anger, as they thought he might, but joined them in pursuit of the chicken. As the fowl cowered under the house, the man yelled to his unexpected guests. He wanted to know how the chicken had gotten loose, and Benjamin said that it had escaped from the wagon when they untied it to wring its neck.

Around and around the house the merry group chased the farmer's chicken.

The Troubadours, the Tragedy

Then the farmer hemmed it himself, and he beamed proudly as he brought it to Benjamin.

"Thank you," said a puzzled Benjamin.

The farmer told them they were lucky not to have had to chase the chicken alone, that he had dozens in the woods but could not catch one without help.

Back on the roadside, the three travelers delighted in their good fortune. They roasted the bird on a spit and, as Nathan strummed the banjo, they all sang again.

Three or four years after, Ray—now in his twenties—stopped by a store near Bluff City, Tennessee. There a half-blind and older friend hailed him. He asked if Ray had any acid wood.

"Yiah, I got three or four cords already split on the mountain above our place," said Ray.

The friend said he could not cut wood in the mountains near his home because there had been a big snow, and deep drifts prevented his bringing chestnut timber down to his truck.

Ray knew that the man, who was called Alf, drove a truck despite eyesight problems. Alf could negotiate roads fairly well except in fog and snow; he drew a pension for his blindness, but he told Ray he would lose his truck if he did not make a payment to the loan company within a week.

"He told me he'd split with me. Said, 'We'll use my gas, my truck, and I'll haul your wood up to Bristol. I'll make the payment on the truck with part of what we sell, and then bring you your half.'"

To himself Ray reasoned: It's my own acid wood, and if I haul it in a rented truck I'll make all the money over the expenses. But Ray "had a feeling" for Alf and also knew his wife, a woman from Beech Creek.

"Well, all right," Ray conceded. "Bring your truck over early tomorrow and we'll go up on the mountain and pick up a load of chestnut wood I've got laying out there."

When Ray arose the next morning he looked out the window and saw cloudless skies. Good. Now Alf would not have to drive through fog and rain. Even on clear days Alf had been known to run off the road; he always saw two roads and would always take the one he saw to his right.

"Besides," says Ray, "Alf was awful bad to drink."

The Troubadours, the Tragedy

— 92 —

Nevertheless, at midmorning Alf arrived.

"He told me that after we loaded up, I could go back with him and spend the night at his house. Said that way, he could pay me on the spot and you won't have to wait for him to bring you the money. Said I could drive, too, both ways."

It was not a good bargain, Ray thought, but Alf's truck would indeed haul a third more acid wood than the rented truck, and there would be no expenses. So he agreed to Alf's proposal.

They spent the morning dragging the chestnut oak logs off the mountain and stacking them high on the truck bed; they arrived at the tannery in time to unload before dark. After they were paid, Alf asked Ray to drive to a grocery store.

"He said him and his wife didn't have much to eat," says Ray. "So, we went to the store where he loaded up with vittles."

In the store his new partner bought food enough, Ray reckoned, to last Alf and his wife, Lessie, a week. That evening Lessie laid out fried ham, gravy, cabbage, beans, and hot biscuits. For breakfast the next morning there were eggs, hominy, and real coffee.

The men then set out for the Beech, both well fed and Ray with twelve one-dollar bills in his jeans. Having stuffed himself at two meals, it occurred to him that helping Alf was not such a bad deal after all.

Before they crossed the line into politically "dry" North Carolina, Alf asked Ray to stop for gas at a small country store. He bought a carton of Little Man Ale, a drink brewed in Tennessee. "Strong drink, it was," Ray remembers. "And Alf put six cans on the seat beside him; didn't take him long—about two cans' worth—to get him a-singing."

Ray thought ahead. If Alf was singing after only two cans of Little Man Ale, he would be in worse shape after drinking it all. How many roads would he see on the drive back to Tennessee?

Over and over Alf sang "Pretty Polly."

"There was a little old man pictured on the beer cans," says Ray. "He was rough, bowed up. Looked like somebody who'd been drinking that beer. If that drink didn't make you sing, there's something wrong with you. It made Alf sing, and, gah, that man could sing."

The memory of Alf suddenly prompts Ray himself to sing:

Pretty, pretty Polly
O yander she stands,

Gild ring on her finger
And lily-white hand.

Pretty Polly, pretty Polly,
Come go along with me,
Pretty, pretty Polly
Come along with me.

Sweet William, sweet William,
I'm a-feared of your ways,
I'm a-feared you'll lead
My poor body astray.

Rode on a little farther
And what did she spy?
A new grave being dug
And a spade a-laying by.

She threw her arms around William
A-pleading to spare her life
Said, I'll go out a-begging
But I won't be your wife.

"Alf was a good man," says Ray. "Nobody thought bad of him a-drinking that Little Man Ale. It brought out the good in him. He'd sing 'Pretty Polly' and would laugh. It made people feel good to hear him.

"Now it reads in the Bible: It ain't what goes in you that spoils you; it's what comes out after it went in. And if it's good in there, or humble, it would bring out the good spirit. If you's evil in there, it makes evil come out. Makes it worser.

"And a lot of people, I've seed 'em, when they wouldn't fight atall sober, but when they get drunk, they'll fight a circle saw a-running. They'd walk on a circle saw with their fists. Gah, I'd get ticked at them. And when they's sober, if you bluff them, they wouldn't fight at all.

"But Alf, he was humble, wouldn't hurt nobody. Got ever so happy when he drunk his Little Man Ale and started singing 'Pretty Polly.'"

When the orders for musical instruments had run their course, Nathan returned to his old cycle of failures. Sadly, too, Frank Proffitt put away his guitar, because the pressure of grubbing a living for Bessie and a growing family did not allow him to follow his musical dreams. At last, sorely needing money, Frank sold the instrument. He had earned it by collecting Arbuckle Coffee coupons.

As the seasons passed, Nathan became an enigma. He would often throw himself into a physical frenzy of farming. He hatched schemes that might turn profitable for his friends but never, it seemed, for him. He came home either dog-tired or heavily sodden with strong drink. Yet for a long time, he still managed to keep the fields trimmed between his place and that of Benjamin and Julie. Whatever his troubles, he never blamed his parents, but at times Rena and the children suffered his abuse.

The day came when the family at last realized that the Nathan of much charm and talent existed only in the past. The Nathan that now emerged left home for days and allowed weeds to take over his fields. He sold humble family possessions; he came home ranting, foul-tongued, and brutish.

He became a man of several personalities. At times he prayed aloud for God to let him live so he could show his worth and virtue; during these periods he would go about the farm singing religious songs. On another day he might turn demonic and morbid. He badgered his son Ray to tell him how a hangman's noose was made.

Early in February 1945, Benjamin died. In the days that followed, Nathan brooded. His life's prop had been kicked away, and he talked but sparingly. He hummed old ballads and gazed for long spells across the winter fields to the east and across the ice-gray mountains.

On the morning of his fiftieth birthday, nearly two weeks later, Nathan left home in a jaunty mood. He told Rena he was going to Banner Elk and would return before dark. But in the late afternoon a deputy sheriff stopped his old car on the road and made his way down the hill, past the springhouse and up to the front door.

The deputy told Rena that Nathan had been found hanging from a crooked chestnut oak along Devil's Highway.

Rena was horrified and disconsolate. Her Nathan, in his wayward moments, had committed unspeakable cruelties; yet he was her husband, the father of her ten living children. No matter how difficult his existence had been, Nathan did

The Troubadours, the Tragedy

not have the right to take a life he had not created, and despite her love for him, she could not accept such a deed. How could the children understand this death? How would Grandmother Julie survive both the loss of her husband and a son within less than two weeks? How could any of them live with the knowledge that Nathan had gone to such lengths to remove himself from their lives?

A clerk in Bob Banner's store later said that a spirited Nathan had come in and paid cash for sixteen feet of rope, exactly sixteen feet. He told bystanders that he would use it to hitch his plow to horses; he would begin spring plowing soon.

Ray was not at home when the deputy arrived. When Nathan failed to return late in the day, he and an uncle had left home to search for him along several miles of the route to Banner Elk. Soon after leaving Andy Hicks Road, they saw what appeared to be two sets of Nathan's footprints in the melting snow. Following the prints, they at last found the body swinging in the wind just beyond the point where a single set of footprints veered off from the roadstead. Mystifying at the time was the fact that, just across the way, a set of identical footprints pointed in the direction of Banner Elk.

Ray sat down to gather himself, but guilt adulterated his sorrow. He remembered how Nathan had joked, asking him how to make a "hangaman's" noose and how much rope was needed. Ray shuddered to remember that he had told his father sixteen feet was normally used for an eight-knot noose. This he had learned from a friend who "studied of such things."

Later Edd Presnell, a neighbor and postman, told Ray that Nathan had been carrying the rope when he rode with Presnell on his afternoon rounds back from Banner Elk. Nathan repeated to Edd that he was planning to use the rope for plowing. At a mailbox near the end of Devil's Highway, a farmer strode up to the car and greeted them in hearty humor; he asked Nathan why he was "bellowing like a bull" when he passed the farm that morning. Suddenly, said Edd, Nathan grabbed the rope, vaulted from the car, and headed back toward Banner Elk. That explained the two separate sets of Nathan's tracks heading in the same direction. One set was made on the morning hike to Banner Elk; the other was made in the afternoon when, after leaving the postman's car, Nathan had made his final walk.

Nathan was buried in the Hicks Cemetery near the fresh mound of his father's grave. A large stone rolled down from the mountain marked his head; a smaller stone lay at his feet. The mourners shivered in icy mountain winds as Rena laid a bouquet of artificial flowers on the coffin. She had fretted because there were no mountain blossoms to pick in February, and this — a gift sent months ago by Anne Warner — was the only floral tribute she could make.

The family slowly trudged home, and the thought came upon Ray that he would now be master of the household, that his duties to his mother and the children would be so heavy that he might never marry.

Nathan Hicks had always thought he might someday beat the odds and climb above the economic privation into which he was born. He had peered over the yoke of the mountains and knew that beyond were people who fared better than he and his kith and kin. He tried mightily to prevail, but the forces of heritage bore down on one side, the realities of life on the other. Perhaps even his last act was an admission of failure; he might have felt unworthy because he could not accept the depth of his family's love for him.

The brooding house on Old Mountain Road today appears almost identical to the yellowed pictures from Nathan and Rena's younger years, except that tall trees now grow between the house and the site where Benjamin and Julie's place stood. In Nathan's day, he had kept the brush trimmed and the saplings cleared so that he could look across at his parents' house and remind himself of a simpler life. In the other direction, he had often climbed the mountain and cleared away vegetation so he could see a stone pinnacle steeped in local legend.

Since he was a boy, Nathan had dreamed of finding lost gold there.

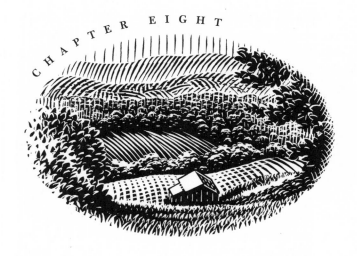

CHAPTER EIGHT

The Day the Earth Moved

By the summer he turned eighteen—nearly five years before Nathan's death—Ray Hicks already knew that legions of outlanders lived better than the people of his own rugged country. He learned the meaning of wealth from oral stories and from books in school. He traveled often to Watauga's county seat and beyond Stone Mountain to Elizabethton. He learned of far-off places like Raleigh and Nashville. He sensed wealth even in the villages he could walk to, such as Valle Crucis, Banner Elk, Boone.

The doctors at the Banner Elk hospital, the Masts of Valle Crucis, the merchants of Boone—all lived better than his kin and neighbors, and Ray knew that few human beings, even among his rural friends, were so poverty-racked as his own family. There were even young ones he had known in school who lived far more comfortably then the Hickses. One was Melvin Shomaker, the second of Bynum and Naomi Shomaker's six children. The Shomakers were by no means wealthy, but Ray reasoned they had never "seed it hard." Ray, on the other hand, had sometimes wondered in his young life if hard times might kill him.

Just a few years back, when he was tending turkeys and singing ballads for his father, it had not occurred to him that millions of ordinary people lived better than his own family. Yet when he sat by the firesides, he had learned of kings and queens, of gold and silver and great castles. In his penniless reality, it was not easy for the boy to understand that riches actually existed, that they were not merely myths from bygone days.

As he grew into his late teens, Ray might have done some thinking about his station in life. His classmate and friend Melvin dwelt on a hillside meadow close to the Balm community; Melvin's father farmed, just as did the Hicks men, but Bynum Shomaker seemed always to dress and feed his family well.

Ray delighted in Melvin's companionship; if his friend enjoyed more comfort than he, so be it. He did not question that others should live a better life. He thought there were no times to come worse than those that had already passed.

"Hard work is my calling," he said. "If something beats me, I say, 'Bless it.' If somebody I know gets more than me, I say, 'Bless them.' "

A critical observer of those days might have seen the Hickses' plight in another light, one of simple economics: The family lived in a remote area; opportunity came their way even less often than it did their neighbors'. The industrious Shomakers and others who lived near the settlement of Balm were exposed to a smattering of commerce not evident in Ray's locale. Balm lay not far outside of Banner Elk, on the road to Valle Crucis. Ray Hicks lived three or four miles north. To reach his home, one had to follow miles of rocky, twisting, dusty roads, then veer off on Old Mountain Road, which ran tortuously to a dead end.

Because the Hickses lived farther from market than the Shomakers, they sold fewer products. Their harvests had to be hauled by oxcarts or mule-pulled wagons over poor roads, whereas the Shomaker farm lay just a half-mile off the paved road between Valle Crucis and Banner Elk. Trucks traveled there from as far away as Savannah and Birmingham. Drivers unhitched their slatted trailers and left them for the Shomakers to load with cabbages.

In her eighty-ninth year, Naomi Shomaker remembers how she and husband Bynum worked together gathering cabbages and loading the truck beds.

"We planted the whole mountainside in cabbage," she says. "We'd get out together and cut the heads from the stems. Bynum was awfully good to cut them. He knew a good cabbage at a glance. He'd cut them and put them in those green cabbage bags, and I held the bags. When he'd get to fifty pounds, I'd know it—I'd held the bags so many times before—and I'd tie it up and take out another one to hold for Bynum."

In the summer of 1940, Ray's friend Melvin was soon to be seventeen. He and older brother Linville helped their parents harvest four or five acres of prime cabbage. Slow mountain rains began in the early days of August, and the skies were constantly overcast. Just enough wetness would be good for the growing cabbages, but after a week or more of rain, Bynum Shomaker grew worried that there could be too much moisture. Yet a good farmer was perpetually concerned about the weather, because it always seemed too wet or too dry.

Bynum was known as a steady worker. He had married Naomi Wallace soon after the First World War, and they soon started a family. Linville was the first-born; then came Melvin, Margaret, Beulah, Joe, and finally Ruby, now sixteen months old.

Bynum was a native of the mountain region, but Naomi had been born in the Oklahoma Territory. Her family had moved there from the mountains before the turn of the century; she was nine when she was brought back to the rich, rolling hills beneath Beech Mountain.

In the way of most mountain men, Bynum took up farming on land owned by his father, John, and they helped each other—Bynum lending brawn and youth, the father providing experience and holdings. From his modest home, Bynum worked the acreage on a great, grassy knoll across the road from his parents' place.

Here eleven-year-old Margaret romped on the grassland above the house; she often scaled the boulders and gazed toward the southwest, where she could see the distinctive profile of Hanging Rock Mountain. But during early August it became difficult for her to play on the granite outcroppings. The rains fell continually, and she could not cross the meadow without soaking her feet.

When it rains for many days in the summer, the insides of even the tightest homes can become mildewed. Clothes develop a moldy smell, and biscuits grow soggy before they can be served.

On the twelfth day of the month, the slow mountain rains changed to torrents, and Naomi gathered the family's clothes to wash them. Then she and young Margaret draped them over the backs of chairs, which they placed close to two stoves in the kitchen. The brick wall behind the stoves would become hot and quickly dry the garments.

Already anxious about his soaked crops, Bynum Shomaker fretted also for the well-being of the people in the valley. Rain came down in silver sheets, and Bynum wondered if the streams might overflow and destroy the bridges. If that happened, he and others living in the Balm section would not be able to travel to Valle Crucis to the northeast or Banner Elk to the southwest. The trucks could not reach his cabbage fields, nor could farmers get to the mercantile stores.

The homes of both Bynum and his father were well distant from Crab-orchard, Shawneehaw, Dutch, and Clark Creeks. There was no danger that floodwaters could climb the hundreds of feet to the great meadow knoll. Still Bynum worried.

The day before, Naomi had baked a cake for an expected visit by her sister and brother-in-law from Virginia. They had dropped by earlier and would visit with other kin in the area before returning for a weekend dinner. Naomi stored the cake in the cabinet Bynum had crafted for her.

"My husband was handy about making things. He built the cabinet, fixed a mirror up top, and put in drawers just like my mother had. Pretty. That was where I stored my cake till the guests came."

In late afternoon, Bynum went out to the barn, east of Naomi's vegetable garden. Naomi finished washing clothes and would begin to prepare supper as soon as her husband brought in dry oak wood for the cooking stove. Melvin was at his grandparents' house below the road; Linville was working in the apple orchard. For the time, there were no men to fetch water; so when the rain momentarily slacked, Naomi took a bucket and waded to the spring.

Rain stood in the meadow above Naomi's ankles, and she marveled that the water appeared clear, as though it flowed from the spring. On the way back to the house, she saw the chickens gathered wet and cold under a tree. She put down the pail of water in the kitchen and went to the bedroom to get a coat. It was around five o'clock, and on her trip from the spring she had felt strong winds and a new chill in the rainy air. She decided then to return to the outside, raise the coop, and let the chickens come in from the weather.

Leaving the bedroom, she pulled on Melvin's jacket. Little Joe, who would be five in October, came up behind her. Baby Ruby slept in her crib in the kitchen. Joe wore new overalls, and in the big pockets he proudly carried a pencil and a small comb his father had given him. Naomi turned to him and said, "The bedroom is getting cold; you'd better come out to the warm kitchen." Then suddenly the house darkened.

"Lord have mercy," she cried.

Bright and amiable Ed Chappell lived on his family's land about three-fourths of a mile north of the knoll. He was twenty-eight, and his wife had given birth to a boy in May. In early August she developed pneumonia and was taken to the hospital in Banner Elk. This afternoon, Ed and his wife's mother had just re-turned from a visit to the hospital when a great roar caused the house to shake. There had been no thunder all day, just continual gusts of heavy rain. When the noise died, showers and wind came in fits.

Between five-thirty and six, a neighbor came by; he told Chappell that the long roll of thunder that rumbled over the hollow had not come from lightning.

In the barn, Bynum Shomaker picked up an armful of newly chopped dry wood and, with his hip, edged open the barn door; it was then that he heard a roar so deafening that he could not discern its direction. Instinctively he turned toward his family's little house. He knew that Linville was in the orchard and that Melvin was down the hill with his grandparents. He had seen Naomi go to the spring earlier and return to the house with a pail of water. Now she would be snugly inside with the smaller children.

Down the long slope, John Shomaker, his wife, and grandson Melvin were shaken by an unworldly noise. They looked aghast toward Bynum's place, but their stares went past the house and up the knoll. What they saw terrified them. Out of the soft, lush meadow, a hideous wall of blackness spouted into the sky like a geyser.

In the barn, Bynum had been shaken by the explosion; his eyes quickly swept up the knoll to where the whole earth came rushing downward. In hor-ror he watched the ground slide past the barn toward the little house. Full-grown trees bobbed like ducks on a rippling river; enormous boulders rolled with the swift, thick current. Such force never before seemed possible, and it focused its intensity upon Bynum's home.

On it came in a path wide enough to engulf the dwelling; then it slammed into the house and spun it around. Before Bynum's eyes the small abode crum-bled. Bricks, glass, and lumber were swallowed up. Only parts of the roof could be seen as a swiftly moving wall of earth, trees, and stones submerged the wreckage. Then the flow divided, rushed like molten lava over the road, skirted the elder Shomakers' home, and fell off to the hollows on either side.

Ed Chappell's neighbor told him that the roar heard all around had come from a mysterious eruption on the great knoll. He said a dwelling had been washed away. Chappell wanted to help, but he knew he could not reach the knoll by following the water-covered roads; on foot, he rushed to nearby homes to gather helpers.

Soon Chappell and several young men made their way across soaked fields and hilly meadows. When they reached the great knoll they found the benumbed Shomaker men sorting through the wreckage.

The rescuers did not understand just what had happened, but the house was gone and the land lay differently. Some speculated that natural gas rose from deep in the earth, exploding when it hit the air. Others said the strange upheaval occurred because so much rain had fallen in so little time.

Bit by bit they began to learn the facts: Like a colossal blotter, the spongy earth rose and swelled to accommodate the excessive moisture, but finally no more could be contained. The torrents of the day built tremendous pressure against the underlying granite, and the subterranean reservoir that had formed higher on the knoll found weak spots and shot through the surface like an oil gusher. So much water gorged into so little space that the earth's crust truly exploded.

Strangely, Naomi Shomaker did not hear the eruption. She knew only that night came instantly. From the barn, Bynum saw the house dance like a poplar leaf in a wildly rushing river. Inside, just moments before, Naomi had slipped on a coat at the bedroom door. Then she heard the baby cry from its crib and felt the floor move beneath her. Even before the building crumbled, Naomi was mauled into half-consciousness.

Daughter Margaret was shaking out the freshly washed garments and placing them on chairs. Both stoves roared, and hot bricks covering the common flue quickly dried each batch. Suddenly Margaret sensed the house turning and saw the heater pitch toward her. She writhed under the awful pain of the stove's burn, the searing of the fiery bricks.

Through gloaming and pain, Naomi thought she saw her baby in its crib as the moving earth bore them both eerily along with the water, the stones, the trees, and the wreckage from the house. Its force carried her on over the old road, where Bynum at last found her. He knelt and kissed her; then he and his brother cradled her on a quilt and carried her to his father's house. They laid her upon a bed in a back room; by that time anxious friends crowded the house.

The Day the Earth Moved

Margaret lay in the middle of the road, imprisoned in a morass of mud, rock, and tree limbs. She did not understand the events that had brought her there. With a free arm she pushed kitchen pots and pans from her face; then with greater effort she raked away the bricks that had burned her skin. Moving her head and eyes, she looked about. Her home was gone. Boulders, brush, and mud surrounded her, but she could see that her grandparents' house still stood.

Melvin passed within a few feet. He was wringing his hands and crying, looking down, apparently searching for the baby. Margaret felt alone and forsaken in her appalling pain. Glass or some object of blind force had torn her flesh to the bone above the left knee. She thought she cried out, but no one answered. Perhaps she called as one screams in a nightmare, when no sound comes. She could not comprehend, and she wondered: What has happened? What has gone wrong?

She saw her father at a distance up the hill. He was bending down and did not notice her; later she would realize he was helping her mother. To the young schoolgirl the suffering seemed to be a bad drama played out in failing light; it lasted a long time.

Then Grandpa Shomaker came down the old road. Margaret lay helpless under the weight of the wreckage, but she could see her grandfather, and he seemed dazed. She thinks she called out to him. He came over and began to pull on her free arm but could not dislodge her from the storm's dregs. Then an uncle reached them. "John, oh John," he cried. "Let's not do that; we've got to move this weight off her first." After the debris was removed, the grandfather lifted Margaret and carried her to his house a hundred yards away.

In the elder Shomakers' house, Naomi lay torpid and bewildered. She remembered Bynum kissing her, but from the time she drew on the coat in her now-destroyed home—when night seemed to come quickly and she called to her God for mercy—she saw the world only as whirling, shadowy forms of no meaning. Through the low babble from the sitting room she heard someone say, "The little girl Beulah is dead."

Now gentle Letha Gwaltney slipped into the room. She took her neighbor Naomi's hand and spoke to her: "It's going to be all right now, Naomi."

"Letha, I want you to pray for me."

Word of the tragedy raced quickly through the farms that stretched along Shawneehaw Creek. Women came with food and good intentions. Men—those who could cross the bridgeless watercourses—brought lanterns and flashlights

The Day the Earth Moved

to search for the missing. By dark, only baby Ruby remained lost. Little Joe—though bleeding, bruised, and dazed—had survived. His head and lip were cut and his teeth loosened. Now he sat in the living room and cried, not comprehending the tragedy. It was a time of vagueness and anguish, but even through his discomfort the boy realized that his treasured comb and pencil were gone.

The storm abated. If this indeed was the edge of a hurricane, as some said, it had come at the worst time. Creeks and rivers had already overrun their banks and rampaged through the valleys. Hardly a bridge or gristmill in the whole region was left standing. Besides the saturated ground and overflowed basins, mysterious earthen explosions had also occurred high on other slopes. Building one's house well away from a stream did not ensure safety. But how was one to know? Never in living memory had water heaved the earth with such force in these mountains, and there was no word for such a strange occurrence. It quickly became known as a "bustout."

Shawneehaw Creek rises from two points located above four thousand feet on the eastern side of Beech Mountain. On the high slopes, one can easily cross the stream by leaping from stone to stone. Within a half-mile, however, its contributing streams fall rapidly southward until they cross the Banner Elk–Valle Crucis road to join Shawneehaw proper. From there the water flows into the Elk River. The western prong of Shawneehaw runs down the mountain behind Ed Chappell's homeplace.

The steep fall of the creek had prevented it from spreading over the adjoining Chappell land, but the Shawneehaw carried such volumes in its rapids that when it reached the foot of Horsebottom Ridge it fanned over the valley, covering crops and roads. Therefore, reckoned Chappell, he and the other volunteers could not reach the Shomaker place by vehicle; all the roads ran through valleys and gaps along the same course as the rampaging streams.

The volunteers finally reached the John Shomaker place on foot, just after Naomi, Margaret, and Joe had been found alive. They did not immediately join in the search for the baby but instead set to work planning ways to get Naomi and Margaret to the hospital at Banner Elk.

It was obvious that Naomi was badly hurt. With so many bones no doubt shattered, she could not move. Margaret, too, could not walk and would need

The Day the Earth Moved

the help of doctors. Oddly enough, her deeply gashed leg had bled little, probably because it was packed with gravel and mud. But her left arm and shoulder were badly burned from the stove that had tilted forward onto her. Her grandmother, working to prepare Margaret for the trip to the hospital, began cutting away the left sleeve of the girl's dress. Burnt flesh came off with the cloth.

Wide, solid boards would be needed upon which to strap mother and daughter. Ed Chappell suggested to Grandpa John that they remove two doors from the tool shed. The rescuers took down the doors, covered them with quilts, and lifted the victims onto their makeshift litters.

The young men, physically hardened by their labors in cabbage and potato fields, grasped the corners of each door. They could not go by way of the flooded roads, so they would wade across the Shawneehaw feeder at its most favorable spot and then climb two hundred feet over the peak of a small mountain.

One of Ed's cousins, Paul Chappell, volunteered the use of his flatbed truck, which was parked in Balm across the mountain. The rescuers would load the victims on the truck and attempt to ford the water on the big road that ran along the Shawneehaw and into Banner Elk.

It was now dark, and the men took turns holding lanterns as they bore the litters through mud and over slippery flat granite. They scaled the grassy mountaintop, and when they descended to the settlement they waded through knee-deep water. Finally they reached the truck and laid the victims head-forward on its open bed. Naomi's uncle, Jim Michael, knelt beside her, and another relative anchored Margaret's litter.

Paul, pleased that his truck cranked despite so much dampness, started the slow drive toward the hospital. As a native of the area, he thought he knew every foot of road from memory, but the old Ford's headlights showed no trace of the road, only the apparent vastness of the flood. Shawneehaw Creek had spread over the route so completely that the lantern lights illuminated only an immense lake. Paul knew to expect hidden dips in the submerged road. He had traveled every day over this same route and remembered at least one declivity where water surely would reach the victims lying in the high truck bed.

The engine labored heavily against the rising water, and the young driver constantly measured with his eye any landmark that appeared above the flood. He saw Mount Calvary Church on the right and gauged its distance from the road as he remembered it. As the water deepened, Paul told Ed, who sat next to him in the cab, that the engine must be kept running, that the absence of pressure would allow the water to siphon into the exhaust pipe and instantly stall the truck.

Just inside the town, the road dipped to its lowest point, and a swash rose high along the vehicle's sides. Ed Chappell looked back and saw by reflected light that Jim Michael and another volunteer were struggling to lift Naomi's and Margaret's heads above the water's new level. Seeing that the water now threatened to inundate the whole truck, Ed quickly clambered through the passenger window, thinking only that he must help keep the victims' heads clear of the water.

With one hand he gripped the door frame; with the other he reached for the truck bed. He strained but could not swing himself from the door to the bed without dropping his legs fully into the water. With the truck continuing to move forward, as he knew it must, he let go his hold on the door and attempted to grab a bed stanchion with both hands, but his shoes, clothing, and slicker created a dragging force; he managed to hold on briefly with one hand before the vehicle's motion yanked him off into the murky flood.

As Ed thrashed in the dark water, Paul continued driving forward, not knowing his cousin had been torn from the truck. Water spumed off the radiator as from the prow of a ship in a storm. As the men in the truck bed strained to keep the heads of Naomi and her daughter above the water's surface, they could not know of Ed Chappell's sudden fight to survive. He struggled against the encumbrances of shoes and clothing to keep his head clear of the flood. As the truck forged ahead, Chappell realized that somehow he had to overtake the moving vehicle.

Fifty years later, recalling the incident in his comfortable home off Shawneehaw Creek, Chappell still could not explain how he managed to propel himself, fully clothed, through the deep waters to reach the truck and to pull himself aboard.

Well past dark, the makeshift ambulance reached the hospital. There Naomi and Margaret were bathed, sedated, and placed in the same room.

The next morning, Ed Chappell returned early to the pitiful scene on the knoll to help look for baby Ruby. About an hour before noon, the search party found the dead child three hundred yards down the mountain. She was still in her crib, covered with mud and lodged under a boulder so big that John Shomaker's ox had to be brought down to pull it off her body.

The Day the Earth Moved

At the hospital, Naomi Shomaker lay in the grayness of half-life—her spine, pelvis, ribs, clavicle, and one leg shattered and her left ear smashed. For many hours she lay in pain, waiting for the small, overwhelmed hospital staff to treat her. She then reckoned she must be too mutilated to live, and this was why no one had come to repair her broken body. On Thursday morning, needing answers, she rang for the nurse and asked for Doctor Tate, of whom she was fond.

"I want you to ask Doctor Tate to come in here," she told the nurse. "I must talk with him."

She wanted the truth. Her daughter Margaret lay in the same room, her mangled leg now sewn and immobilized. It seemed mysterious to Naomi that no physician had come to her own bed. Had she not been hurt worse than her daughter? Yet Margaret had been treated but Naomi had not. If, on the other hand, she was beyond medical help, she would send for her family so that she might speak to them all for the last time.

"If there's nothing they can do for me," she told the nurse, "let me know now."

"Oh, honey," the kindly nurse answered. "You're going to be fine; I can hear the stretcher coming now."

Since her birth out west, Naomi's black tresses had never been cut. When combed out, the hair reached well below her hips and she could sit on it; but now she learned that thirty-seven years of its growth would have to be cut away.

After her broken bones had been refitted, Naomi was placed in a cast from neck to toes. She remained in the hospital for three months.

The landslide that carried away the Shomaker house was one of scores that occurred that day. Sixteen mountain inhabitants died in bustouts and floods. Crops were ruined, livestock drowned, bridges washed out, and gristmills disintegrated.

There were as yet no devices to predict hurricanes, but information gathered after the fact said that a hurricane spawned in the Caribbean had come inland over South Carolina and then up into the North Carolina mountains, dumping heavy rains upon the already soaked region. Some say that the tempest passed into Kentucky somewhere, but then doubled back to North Carolina before it died. In Watauga, the still-furious wind and rain broke down the earth's defenses.

From that month forward, mountain life was never the same. Not only had

The Day the Earth Moved

the titanic storm ruined property and taken lives; when it swept away water-powered mills, wooden bridges, and crops, it took with it years of work, and for many it tarnished trophies of upward flight.

When the narrow-gauge tracks of the beloved Tweetsie locomotive were washed out along the Watauga River, directors of the Linville River Railway decided that the line to Boone would be abandoned. Those who lived within hearing distance of Tweetsie thought of the little train as their own, and they missed the lonely sound of its whistle. For many years it had run between Boone and Johnson City, carrying mine ore, lumber, and a few passengers. Although the train would still travel between Tennessee and the iron mines of Cranberry, it would never again pass down the Watauga Valley.

On the afternoon of the storm, Ray Hicks and his older brother Lewis looked fearfully in the direction of the booming sounds coming off Beech Mountain. What strange thing was taking place?

"It was popping and exploding all around," Ray remembers. "One bustout started right up yander, right where we could see it coming out of the ground; if it hadn't popped when it did—hadn't let the water out—it would have brought down part of the mountain on us. It moved a boulder big as my house . . . *moved* it, the water did. Got beneath it, undercut it, and scooted that rock about sixty feet and left a big trench there.

"Gah, that water'd fly and roar. See, the water seeped down deep in the rocks and didn't have a place to go; then more rain came and caused pressure to build down there. The whole earth was just full of water. Hit was a-going everywhere, just pushing out and making sounds like thunder."

Many a mountain farmer, plowing his bottomlands the next spring, found new boulders in his fields—the same stones that before had lain on the hillside.

Ray recalls that, on the sides and tops of mountains, granite formations knifed through the soil and created new outcroppings. They sculpted rugged images, and their shadows formed different patterns as the sun moved across the sky.

"The earth's been changing like that since time began," Ray observes. "But all of it is in patterns of God's purpose. Yiah. God fixed it like that. To change. They ain't necessarily any difference in what God did and what our scientists think.

The Day the Earth Moved

"Now, you take that rock right up yander on the mountain. If we'd seed that rock when it was first there, it'd be a lot different probably. The weather beat it and froze it and thawed it over millions of years. The rock was maybe twice or three times the size we see it today. Pieces of it crumbled off and gave us chemicals to make the plants grow . . . to make the food and grass and trees grow. See, everything makes topsoil. I once heard that it took a million years to build a inch of topsoil. A million years to build an inch."

He points to a stone the size of a wagon. It is anchored in the soil above his house. When his father first planted there, he harvested larger potatoes near the boulder than anywhere else in his field. Around stones, Ray says, one finds nature's plant foods, leeched out of the rocks through the ages.

Back on the great knoll, Melvin and his brother Linville began new lives. Their mother would remain in the hospital for a long time. Little Joe, now staying at his grandparents' home, did not understand the events that had occurred; he knew only that he missed his mother and that things were not the same.

Margaret came home from the hospital a few weeks before her mother, but she remained out of school for a while. Her teacher was Marshall Ward, a man the Shomakers would always adore. Every schoolday he came by to bring Margaret her assignments, staying to tutor her. After Margaret was able to return to classes, she still could not climb aboard the bus, so Ward would stop by in the mornings to take her to school and then bring her home in the afternoons.

Across the way, Letha Gwaltney prepared meals and snacks for Bynum and his volunteer helpers as they worked to build a new home. Ed Chappell and his wife looked in almost every day, and at harvest time women of the settlement came and helped Bynum cut cabbages. Marshall Ward brought a horse, and young Linville paired it with the Shomakers' own horse to make a wagon team. Linville would take the horses into the fields and load cabbages onto wagons to be taken to market.

When Naomi was well enough to leave the hospital, her husband and Ed Chappell came for her. They had brought pillows to soften the ride home, but Doctor Tate told them Naomi would need sturdier support. He said she would remain an invalid for a long time. The men drove home and spent much of the day anchoring a bunk to the bed of the truck. Then they returned to the hospital, and this time the doctor approved the makeshift ambulance. Bynum and Ed eased Naomi onto the bunk and drove her slowly home.

Soon after, Bynum took his wife to their new white house by the side of Lee Gwaltney Road. Its construction was a testament to a Watauga country tradition. Men and women had freely given money and labor to help Bynum build it. He recounted to Naomi the events since the bustout.

"We'll never be able to repay them," he said.

Naturally a small woman, Naomi weighed only seventy-five pounds after the ordeal. Bynum carried her from the car and into all the rooms, one by one, and showed her every amenity.

As soon as Naomi was able to sit up, Ed Chappell's young wife came over. She brought her six-month-old son and laid him on Naomi's lap.

"I shall never forget the moment," Naomi says.

On a crisp November morning more than fifty years later, Naomi and Margaret are driven slowly along Devil's Highway under the great knoll where the bustout occurred. Down the hill, only a tall stone chimney stands to mark the place where Bynum's parents lived. They are dead now, as are Bynum, Linville, and Melvin. The knoll is a quiet place of uncommon beauty. People pass and admire the landscape where Bynum raised cabbages and where Margaret played upon the great stones. Almost nobody living knows that up the slope, where one can see Hanging Rock Mountain, there are scars in the earth remaining from a long-ago subterranean cataclysm.

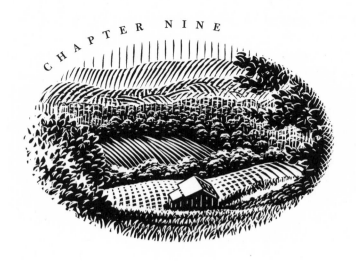

CHAPTER NINE

Too Young to Leave Her Mother

He was lanky and awkward and he talked in a strange way. Since he was six or seven, he had tinkered with any mechanical thing he could find on the farm. He memorized the workings of his father's Model-T, and he studied the way houses were built.

When he grew up, Ray Hicks liked to talk. As a boy he had listened, drinking in retellings of the past. As his grandparents narrated, he formed visions of long-ago times. "Across-the-water" fantasies etched deep pathways into a curious chamber of memory. Even in advanced age he effortlessly recalls hundreds of ballads and rare tales.

He was uncommonly bright, even though he had lagged behind his classmates in numbers and letters at the free school. He forfeited a chance at good primer learning because he had a "feeling" to stay home and help his mother. He worked when he might have been in school. As he aged, he reached into his vast store of fables to entertain people, to tell about the old life.

That would be his calling.

As Ray grew, he came to understand the foibles of his parents and, though he might complain to them, he steadfastly helped them, never once thinking of not loving them. Also, he recognized their gifts. Though Rena leaned upon him for house chores and for tending the younger children, it was from her that Ray learned compassion and gentleness, learned to fear God. From industrious Nathan, the developing boy learned to equate an idle day with laziness. From Rena's weaknesses grew his determination to be strong, from Nathan's excesses his vow to be moderate.

On Sunday nights he stole looks at the girls in church and wished secretly to be with them. But like many mountain people, Ray shunned impudence; he failed to step forward when at times a standoffish girl might have liked him to be bold. Often, when one girl spurned him, he backed away from them all. He was introspective and reckoned he was too tall and too different to be attractive. Many times he admired a mountain flower that he did not reach to pick.

His friends tried to keep Ray socially active; if they had not, he would have stayed at home all the time—working by day and playing his harmonica by night. Occasionally friends would persuade him to visit neighbor girls, but he was never sure of himself; his insecurities alone caused rejection, and he developed notions of unworthiness.

Once he met a comely girl from a poor family nearby. To make money to buy clothes for her, Ray gathered herbs and cut haw in addition to his daily work. For three years he "went with" the girl. He talked of making a life with her, and she would tell him they must put off marriage a little longer. Ray wanted to wed and settle down, but at last the girl broke off the courtship.

One Sunday Ray walked over to Beech Creek to visit a colorful old mountain orator and sometime preacher. The man, whose wife had died, lived alone in an old shack. Ray felt God's presence in the man and never knew him to do one unholy thing. He gloried in the man's speech and thought him to be an oracle of the past. That is why Ray had sought his company this very day. When he knocked on the preacher's door he was feeling despondent and defeated. He did not want to admit he was there to forget the girl who had "throwed me aside," but after spending much of the afternoon with the old man, Ray felt refreshed and cheered.

He left the shack and was about to cross the creek when he saw several boys and girls walking together along the road. Among them was a comely, blue-eyed girl whom he knew to be from the area. The strollers stopped to talk. They were just wandering and did not appear to be paired up, and; they invited Ray to join them. As they sauntered along the creek, Ray moved up beside the pretty girl and spoke:

"I don't know you too well, but will you walk with me?"

Yes, the girl replied, she would walk with him.

As they ambled along, the girl stopped and addressed the group. She said an old woman, Molly Lee, lived up on Beech Mountain. She would tell all their fortunes if one of the boys had a nickel to spend.

The boys laughed. One said if he had a nickel he'd think he was rich. Ray fished into his pockets. He at times worked in the sawmills and tried to keep his pockets from being empty, "just to know I was worth something." He found nothing, and they all laughed at their lack of wealth. As they resumed walking, Ray absently rummaged through his pockets again; this time he came up with a buffalo nickel, "one I'd mis-felt the first time." Instantly he was the center of importance.

The group was not sure Ray should spend his only nickel on a fortune telling, but Ray told them:

"I'd spend five dollars on you if I had it."

The adventure promised to break the tedium of a sleepy afternoon. The newfound nickel brightened the restless group's spirits, and they set out to find the house of Molly Lee.

"It was a way to have some fun," says Ray. "A way to be together."

The party walked three miles up an old wagon road. When they arrived, the girls knocked and were presently invited into the house. The boys waited.

"The girls wanted to see what was ahead of us," says Ray. "For, gah, now people like that Molly Lee knowed things. Them people could read your mind."

Then the girls beckoned from the door for the boys to come into the large, unpainted house, one that reminded Ray of his own homeplace. Here, in the dark and disquieting interior, they met an old woman in a long dress, button-down shoes, apron, and—though she had not been outside all day—a bright yellow bonnet.

Soon the fortune telling began. The woman put coffee grounds into a cup and presented it to one of the nervous visitors. Giggling, the girl did as directed and turned the cup upside down. Rivulets formed along the inside of the cup; coarse grounds shaped patterns in its bottom. The girl squealed delightedly when told a handsome suitor would come to her. Then the other girls took turns. They laughed and hid blushing faces when they heard that babies or strange men were in their futures. Then the boys, bashful and reluctant, took their turns; Ray was the last of them.

"We all was a little scared," says Ray. "Some people didn't want their fortunes ever read because it might be too bad—and they didn't want to know. But Molly Lee wouldn't tell you if she thought it was too bad. Didn't want to hurt you."

When Ray's turn came, Molly Lee poured the coffee grounds into the cup.

"I turned the cup, rolled it around in my hands, and she looked in it. She blowed her breath a little. She said, 'My God, young man, you've been having troubles, a troubled mind, and you're working too hard. It shows here that you work too hard and don't go courting.'

"Said I was smart, and that made me feel big . . . me there with that beautiful girl. She said, 'Whoever you air, you're smart in mind, and you help a lot of people.' "

The woman was silent as she peered intently into the cup, then looked up again:

"She told me," says Ray, "that the coffee grounds showed her that I'd went with a fair-haired girl and bought her clothes. Thought I was gonna marry and settle down; but the girl let me go."

How did she know? the boy wondered.

"In my mind, gah, I got kinda scared of her. And Molly Lee said, 'Now here it is . . . in the cup.' She let me look, but I couldn't see anything but coffee grounds. And she says, 'Here it is: You *can't* get married, young man.'

" 'Oh. Why?'

"And she told me, said, 'Well, there's a dark-haired little girl, lives back over yander. I can see she lives in a little old box house where groundhog hides are nailed to the sides. Little old rough house. Oh, look, young man. She's a pretty one, the girl that's supposed to be your wife. But you can't marry her.' "

Ray was perplexed: The girl was supposed to be his wife, but he could not marry her. Why?

" 'She's too young,' she told me. 'Too young to leave her mother. She's somebody you don't know.' "

Ray nodded yes, but he did not comprehend. A young stranger, she was. Too young.

" 'You'll have to wait for her to get older,' Molly Lee said."

Too Young to Leave Her Mother

A young man under the Beech did not despair when it took him some time to find a bride. Commonly, a family tried to keep sons at home to help with crops and chores until they were twenty-five. Daughters were "married off" between the ages of fifteen and eighteen. Spinsters were liabilities; bachelors, assets.

Even so, mothers worried when their sons were not inclined toward courting. Rena appreciated Ray, and she needed his help to rear the young ones. But she would have been happier if Ray had showed some interest in getting away from home. Soon all the eligible girls would be gone, but still Ray stayed home. He helped bring up the younger Hicks brood and bore the brunt of farm chores; he often worked so long and hard that he fell asleep before supper.

"It was hard. No money. And so I just settled down at home. I figured I can't get married. I'd had a rough time getting a girl I liked. And I just forgot Molly Lee's fortune-tale. I just quit."

He stopped going out on Saturdays and Sundays, and his face was often covered with stubble. He stayed home and helped his mother.

"Mama'd say, 'Ray, you ought to clean up some,' and I'd say, 'No, I'm quit. I'm give up.' My mind thought I was meant to stay at home and work like a slave for whatever time I lived."

His young twenties were quickly passing. One day he was up on the mountain, busy at work, when a low, sweet voice spoke to him:

Ray, go down to your house. Clean up and shave. Go to the meeting at Cool Springs—a gathering in the old wood church there.

Ray was not much alarmed. The whispering Voice had spoken to him before. If he did as it suggested, problems seemed to solve themselves.

When he finished his work, he went home and heated spring water on the cook stove, took the kettle into his room, and poured water into a galvanized wash tub. He bathed and shaved, then put on new overalls, clean shirt, suit coat, and a brimmed hat. His mother smiled when she saw him. He told her he would be going to the meeting at the church.

He walked alone to the meetinghouse. Inside, men sat on the right, women on the left, with an aisle down the middle. Normally the young men would look for a seat on the back rows, but Ray had learned at churches over on the Watauga River to sit down front. Tonight, however, he was late; he slipped quietly into the meeting and seated himself beside his male friends. It was a section the preacher called "the devil's corner."

In many churches there was no singing, but here in Cool Springs the Baptists sang heartily. Women made up most of the choir, and lanky Ray could see them clearly over the heads of the congregation. The choir led the group in songs he knew well—tunes like "May the Circle Be Unbroken." Ray sang loudly.

After the opening prayer and song, the minister mounted the pulpit and preached a long sermon. Ray listened only at intervals. At other times he thought of the Voice on the mountain. There must be a reason it had told him to clean up and come to the meeting.

The preacher droned on, and in the devil's corner Ray's friends fidgeted and whispered. Ray kept part of his attention on the preacher and part on the choir, where he had noticed a young girl with dark eyes. Her black hair was plaited and her skin was the color of milk cream.

The preaching finally ended and the choir stood to sing. Under the flicker of coal-oil lights, Ray watched the pretty girl. Then the Voice spoke again:

Ray, that's your wife.

Can't be, Ray thought. It's that I'm imagining the Voice. But he hearkened back to old Molly Lee's saying over her coffee grounds: "You'll have to wait."

Years had passed since the old woman had told him the girl was too young to marry. Now that same little girl would be older. The choir girl—the one with the dark eyes and creamy skin—could she be that girl? His heart thumped and he felt blood rise in his cheeks. The Voice had told him to come to the meeting-house, and now it had spoken again:

That's your wife.

"And the feeling hit me," says Ray. "I didn't think anymore like I was quit. I felt good when I looked at the girl. She was not too young for me, now. I couldn't believe how pretty she was to look at."

Full dark came, and the night was filled with the sounds of a mountain summer. The assemblage filed slowly out of the church and the lamps inside were flicked off one by one. Only the headlights of rickety vehicles illuminated the grounds. Ray, still emboldened by the Voice, was of a mind to ask the girl if he could walk her home, wherever she lived.

Then Will, a friend from the devil's corner, came alongside. Ray told him he was looking to walk with one of the choir girls, who no doubt would be strolling home in a group. Would Will come along? For a time the boys could not find the girls in the dim glow of headlights; then Will spotted four of them seated on

Too Young to Leave Her Mother

chairs in the bed of the deacon's pickup truck. The young girl was among the riders.

As the vehicle moved away, Ray and Will ran behind it. Engine sounds and the truck's loud rattles masked the sound of the boys' approach. As the truck slowed down to ford a nearby branch, the boys caught up and tried to leap onto the back bumper. The girls, facing forward, did not see or feel the action. Will landed squarely on the bumper and grasped the tailgate; Ray, too, clung to the tailgate, but one foot slipped forward so that it was lodged between the bumper and the truck bed. With his free foot he hopped on the road as he tried to wrench the other foot from its trap.

He did not yell out. As the truck pulled away from the creek bed and gained speed, Ray hopped faster. Will was not aware of his friend's predicament, since he had turned and was squinting to see the girls now silhouetted by the truck's faint headlights. Ray felt he could go no further, but still he did not shout. As the truck's speed increased again, he managed to pull his trapped leg free. Will did not see Ray drop from the vehicle; he was still looking toward the girls.

Finally, at a point near the schoolhouse, Will turned to see that Ray was no longer hanging on. As the truck gained new momentum, the concerned Will clumsily jumped off. He hit the roadside with stupefying force and lay semi-conscious, his clothing torn, his knees and elbows cut and bruised. Minutes later Ray caught up with his dazed friend. Will had been thrown through a chestnut fence.

Ray scolded him: "You shoulda waited until the truck slowed at the next fording place. You shoulda not jumped."

Thus their inglorious adventure ended. Luckily, Ray thought, the girl with ivory skin and dark tresses had not seen the debacle. Ray and his limping friend made their way home in the dark. Each promised that if they were ever to meet the girls from Matney, they'd not do it by stealing a ride on a pickup truck.

Yet the echo of the Voice reverberated:

That's your wife.

Back at the homeplace, Ray thought often of the girl with skin like risen cream and hair that shone like raven feathers.

Sunday morning rolled around, and Ray again went to the meetinghouse and sat in the devil's corner. Across the length of the church he stared at the pretty girl in the choir. When the last amen had been said, Ray rushed from the church hoping to intercept the girl before she climbed into the pickup truck to be taken home by the deacon and his wife. To his delight, the truck was nowhere to be seen.

The girls came out of the church and began walking in the direction of Matney. Near the creek that flowed by the Ward and Farthing farms—where the two boys had clambered aboard the truck several nights before—Ray caught up with the girls. He walked beside the one whom the Voice had said would be his wife. Close to her in the light of day, Ray saw that the girl was as lovely as she appeared in the choir. She was silent and did not lift her face, but at times she cut her eyes from a bowed head as Ray walked beside her.

As the group reached the creek's edge, Ray asked the girl to let him help her across the stones. But like a frightened fawn she leaped across the rocks, and her feet splashed into the water.

"Did you get your feet wet?" Ray called.

"You ought to know I got them wet," the girl answered.

Her words stunned Ray. They were the first she had spoken to him, but he was not discouraged. He caught up with her again and reached for her arm.

"Get that old big hand off me," she demanded.

Instantly the shy Ray gave up. It was clear to him that the dark-haired beauty wanted nothing to do with him. He felt empty, fearful that he must have been mistaken about hearing the Voice; therefore, he would stop his pursuit—even though he had been sure the Voice said he would marry the girl, even though she was the fairest he had ever seen.

Her name was Rosa. She came from a simple farm in a place called Sandy Flat, near Matney. She was too young to know that her fright—a lashing out born of extreme shyness—would discourage her new suitor.

Yet during the next week Rosa thought of the slim boy. She told her sisters she regretted turning him away. He seemed gentle and he had feelings. He was the gangling boy one of her choir friends had said should sing high-do, "because he is so tall."

A married sister, Dorsey, told Rosa that she knew Ray, that he was a kind person, one who worked hard and was good to his mother. Rosa became penitent. If the Hicks boy came to the meetinghouse next Sunday, if he should ask her, she would let him walk her home.

Back at the homeplace, Ray was feeling unworthy. His mother saw that he was retreating into his shell. He dwelled upon his rejection and thought maybe the Voice had played games with him. He reasoned: She is too shy and does not understand. I will not get started with her anymore.

"She didn't know me, and she must have thought of me in the way she'd been teached—to be a-feared of boys. That's the way all mountain girls was taught back then. Boys might do them wrong. That's what parents were afraid of. They didn't want no baby at the knee of a girl that wasn't married.

"Well, with me they didn't have nothing to worry about. I was innocent and knowed it. Couldn't understand how others didn't see that. I wouldn't have harmed any girls and ruint their lives."

Rena watched her son return to his old monastic life. His whiskers grew dark and scraggly; he went back to his former work pattern. All day he tended the animals, dug potatoes, gathered corn and cabbage, chopped trees, and split logs. He did not play his harmonica in the evenings. Then one night one of his sisters came in from a church meeting to find Ray staring at the walls. She told him a black-headed girl in the choir had asked about him.

"Why didn't the tall boy come back to church?" the girl had asked.

Now as Ray worked in the fields, the vision of the young woman often came back, but still the idea of paying court to her had remained subdued because of her brash treatment of him at the creek. He knew there would be a church meeting Saturday night, but he would not go. He would not punish himself again.

But as the meeting night drew nearer, Ray was strangely drawn to the church. He would not attend, he told himself, but he might walk past. It would be good to listen to the choir and to know that the pretty girl would be inside. When Saturday night approached, however, his courage flagged.

In the afternoon he dressed. He strolled over to his uncle's house and bought a half-gallon of grape wine. As he was leaving, Will came along and asked for a taste of the wine. Ray had planned only to nurse the bottle along, to take a sip or two; it would give him courage to walk past the church. But as he walked with his friend one swallow led to another, and soon the boys were buoyed and talkative. Yes, they would indeed walk past the church. If the pretty Rosa came out with her sisters, Ray would stare directly at her, though he had abandoned any thought of courting her.

As the boys made their way toward the meetinghouse, they would occasionally stop and sip from the jug. They dawdled until after dark. The meeting by now would be half over, and they were still a mile away. Before they could reach the church they saw headlights approaching. The deacon's truck! They could see as it turned the bend that girls were again seated in chairs on the truck bed. He did not care for Rosa, Ray told himself; still, he would not want her to see him with the wine jug.

"I jumped across the road to hide the wine. Didn't want them to see the jug shining in the lights. But Rosa and the girls—everybody in the truck—seed me a-trying to hide the wine. And, gah, them girls was teached bad by their mothers about any boys that drunk. They seed me and just figgered I's drunk, just because I was hiding the jug in the bushes."

The deacon's truck rattled past and left the boys ignored and dishonored in the dust. The aloofness was palpable. The deacon's wife looked straight ahead, and the girls all seemed to lift their chins. Ray thought it was unfair: "I wasn't drunk—just sipping the wine."

During the next week, though, his emotions seemed to heal. His courage rebounded, and his resolve never to see Rosa withered. She had asked about him, hadn't she? His sister had told him so. Rosa must be interested, and it was his duty to let her know that he was not drunk when she saw him hiding the wine jug.

While tending the animals and gathering cabbages that week, Ray's daydreams were of the girl. From the house, Rena could hear him as he worked in the field. He whistled and hummed, and there was a new determination about him. At nights he would take out his harmonica and play "John Henry" and freight-train songs. Come Saturday he put on new overalls, a suit coat, and a freshly ironed shirt; Rena tied his tie.

He did not tell his mother where he was going, but he put the harmonica in his bib pocket, placed the felt hat raffishly upon his head, and struck out walking. In his mind, he tried to see Sandy Flat. He would find the place and read the names on the mailboxes. He had already learned that the girl's father was Monroe Harmon, a man he already knew of. It would be a miracle if the girl's house turned out to be the one with groundhog hides tacked to its walls—the one in Molly Lee's vision. He did not admit to himself that the purpose of his outing was to satisfy his curiosities: about Molly Lee's fortune telling of years ago; about the message of the Voice.

A passerby on the rude, winding road might have been heartened by the sight of the six-seven young mountaineer, face scrubbed to an apple's shine, taking long strides and playing a harmonica. In a couple of miles he passed the church; at the creek he took off his shoes and rolled up his pants. After crossing, he traversed the Farthing and Ward properties, turned in the direction of Matney, and plodded merrily along to the place they called Sandy Flat.

When he came within sight of what he hoped was Rosa's home, a boy and girl sat at the crossing gap, a place to allow people (but not sheep and cattle) to pass in and out of a pasture. The girl, he found, was from the church choir; she was the one who had joked that the singers should recruit Ray to sing high-do.

Ray stopped and played his harmonica for the couple. They talked for a while, and as Ray took his leave, he asked where the Harmon girls lived; he wondered if they were at home.

The girl pointed to a distant dwelling, and Ray thought he saw curious spots on its walls. The Harmon girls had been away, but she believed they had returned.

His pulse raced as he turned back to wave farewell to the two at the crossing gap. He was in sight of where the girl Rosa lived. He would not be expected there, and he probably would not be invited in, anyway. But just being there—just seeing the girl's house—was all he would want for that day.

When he neared a bank of mailboxes, he saw the name *Monroe Harmon* crudely printed on one. Then he looked to the nearest house, the one the girl at the crossing gap had pointed out, and he was astounded. For a long moment he stood and stared.

"Gah, there it was! The dark ghosty things I saw on the sides from back yander—they was groundhog hides."

It was a setting not much different from the one he had harbored in his imagination, a vision conjured years ago by Molly Lee, who told him he could not marry then because his destined bride was too young.

Soon he was to find that Rosa Harmon, although nine years younger than he, was now certainly old enough by mountain customs to marry.

On this day he would not see Rosa. But long after he was back home and working in the fields and the sawmill, he thought of the little house at Sandy Flat, the one with the beautiful groundhog hides tacked to the weathered sideboards. He frowned when the thought intruded that both the girl and her family might still think her too young for marriage, but he smiled to think upon Rosa, the girl of the coffee grounds—Rosa, the one appointed by the Voice.

He remembered her at the creek crossing and how her eyes shone like a frightened rabbit's. He would not rush her—his intended catch.

Too Young to Leave Her Mother

Days passed before Ray saw Rosa again. Before they ever dated, the rites of courtship had begun, and there were forces drawing them toward each other. Ray stood outside the house of Rosa's grandfather on the afternoon of a church meeting there, but he would not come inside. When Rosa's sister Dorsey patted the fireplace hearth and motioned through the open door for Ray to come sit beside Rosa, Ray still elected to stay outside. He could not keep his eyes off Rosa as she sat on the hearth holding a younger Harmon child.

When the meeting broke up and the little congregation began to leave, Ray caught up with Rosa.

"Will you let me walk you home?"

Already Rosa knew that shy Abby and her pushy mother, Dory, from Beech Creek had walked to the meeting with Ray. She knew also that as Ray stood in the yard, girls on the porch winked often at him.

"Why don't you ask some of the girls who was winking at you?" Rosa said.

"Well," Ray answered, "I reckon I could get one of them to go with me if I wanted to."

"That'd be all right with me."

Ray walked home alone, but strangely, on the way his hopes began to soar. The meeting with Rosa had not been exactly cordial, but her manner when she refused to walk with him told him she did not want to share him with shy Abby or the winking girls. Perhaps she was still angry because of the wine jug. Even so, her very anger told him she was interested.

He whistled all the way home.

It was on a Saturday when Ray walked over to visit his cousin and friend Floyd, who lived within sight of Rocky Knob on the east side of Laurel Creek. While Ray was there, Monroe Harmon came by. He knew of Ray, but did not know of Ray's interest in his daughter Rosa. As they stood talking in the yard, Monroe asked about Ray's work at home and in the sawmill. He asked about his family. It occurred to Ray that it was a strange world; he had known of Monroe Harmon long before he visited Molly Lee, but until recently he had not known where the man lived or that the girl of Molly Lee's coffee cup was Monroe's daughter. Then Monroe asked Ray's age.

"Twenty-six in August," Ray told him.

Monroe was astonished that he was not married at that age.

Too Young to Leave Her Mother

"No, I can't get married. Failed it every way."

Monroe assured him: From his own daughters, he could let Ray have a wife.

When Rosa learned from Floyd's wife that Monroe had offered her as a bride for Ray, she was furious.

"Papa," she cried defiantly, "you think us girls can't get a boyfriend on our own?"

Throughout the following week, Ray "studied" much about Rosa. He had loved her beauty from the first; now he loved her fiery ways. She would make a spirited wife.

The next Saturday he paid for a haircut, bathed, shaved, put on a second-hand suit, and set out for Sandy Flat. From his sawmill earnings he bought a bag of marshmallows and sticks of licorice. He tucked the candy in his suit coat, held his harmonica in his hand, and walked the long dusty roads to the little house of the groundhog pelts.

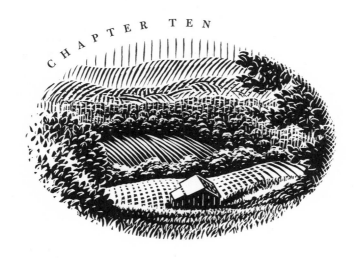

CHAPTER TEN

Triumph of the Omens

Ray was cautious in his pursuit. He did not call on Rosa directly, but whenever he visited the Harmon house he parceled out sweets among all the sisters, the parents, and Grandfather Kell. The adults greeted him openly; the girls were polite but diffident. The Harmon family seemed not to be aware, but they must have understood that the reason Ray Hicks came so steadfastly was to be near Rosa.

It was a good month, October, and as Ray strode toward the Harmons' house he breathed the crisp air and stopped along the rocky road to take in the vaporless, clear view of the far mountains. Clusters of berries glittered on the ash trees, and the green of summer had yielded to yellow, russet, and brown. The previous night, autumn winds had gusted so that foliage was torn from the trees, and Ray saw newly fallen leaves padding the forest floors. November would come, and the bright leaves would wither. Dark and spindly tree forms would eclipse October's brightness, and the mountains would turn somber. Yet not even the bleakness of winter could chill the warmth he felt in the Harmon cottage—especially should young Rosa smile upon him. These were the early days of his serious courting, and he began to love October as no other month.

As Ray approached the little house in Sandy Flat, wood smoke curled skyward in the crisp, chilly air. He called his halloo from a comfortable distance, as mountain people are wont to do. It was old Kell who opened the door to let him in. Ray drew up a straight chair before the mudrock fireplace, and soon the girls came into the room to share the marshmallows and licorice he had brought in brown sacks. Then Ray went outside and stripped dead tree limbs to make spits. Now all of them—grandfather, parents, and daughters—joined the young man at the hearth; the happy group toasted marshmallows over flickering embers.

As fall melded into winter, the Harmons seemed to think of the tall young man not just as a beau for Rosa, but as a friend to them all—a fascinating caller who brought sugars, played a harmonica and banjo, and sang ballads and told stories.

Grandfather Kell became attached to the young man. When he guessed it was time for Ray's arrival, he would draw his chair to the entrance; there he would crack the plank door, peer down the road, and, when he caught site of Ray, fling the portal open and stand to greet him. If a chilly wind of late afternoon blew into the room, the other occupants would just have to endure. The important thing was that Ray Hicks, a new and exotic figure, would be arriving from the distant Old Mountain Road to bring new warmth and life to the Harmon cottage.

It was an onerous exercise, in those days, for a boy to "get started" with a girl. First, most daughters had been warned by their mothers that boys were not good enough, sanctified enough, to approach them. After such injunctions, girls were reluctant to indicate in any way that they spent time thinking of boys, that they wanted their hands held, their lips kissed. They acted shy and might even flee when a strange boy approached. Had not Abby from Laurel Creek run ahead when Ray agreed to go to the church meeting at Kell's house, so that Abby's mother, Dory, had to walk with Ray to salve his feelings? Had not Rosa herself run through the creek in her Sunday shoes rather than let Ray help her across?

"Them girls was shy," Ray says. "Boys would say they had to run them down like a rabbit. Them girls had rabbit blood in them."

Then there was the vigilance of the mothers. Ray recalled that boys had to be careful not to show signs of poor character: drinking and gambling were taboo, and boys had to show industry and self-reliance. For some, it was not possible to please a girl's family, much as they would like to "marry off" the daughter. That is why many a mountain girl and boy eloped before seeking the blessing of her parents.

Triumph of the Omens

Ray wanted to get along. He cared deeply what others thought of him, especially his elders. Moreover, he found that he liked to be with the Harmon family. He would cut Kell's hair, bring storebought sugars, entertain, and glory in the family's admiration. Rosa remained the apple of his eye, but he was satisfied to win her in a subtle way. In those early days of the courtship, when the family was ready to go to bed, Ray would pack his harmonica and banjo and take leave.

As the visits became frequent, an obstacle arose. Young boys from around Matney got wind of Ray's visits. They had picked up the ancient practice of "rocking" swains from other neighborhoods.

"See, there was just so many girls in one place, and the boys living in those parts didn't want outsiders coming in and stealing their girls," Ray relates. "So they'd do awful things. They'd hide behind bushes and trees and throw at them courting boys." If a boy came in a pickup truck, he might later find the tires slashed or sand poured in the fuel tank.

Soon after Ray started coming to the Harmon place, he was confronted by a dozen or more country urchins, some as old as fourteen. They cared not that an outsider was coming into the settlement to take away one of the girls; what they wanted was booty, and they parlayed an old custom to fit their needs. They were young highwaymen — serious trick-or-treaters who demanded candy and chewing tobacco and hurled rocks and sticks when denied their prizes.

In his first encounter, Ray the pacifist tried talking to the boys. But his tormentors became sullen and threatening. Ray realized that they were too young for him to fight, that even if he had been an explosive man he could not attack boys so young. To pacify them, he promised treats when he came again.

On the next visit, he carried two sacks: one with goodies for the Harmons; another filled with tobacco and gum for the miniature outlaws. He established dominance at the outset. He set up rules and the boys acquiesced. Ray would not be responsible for distribution. The ransom would be presented to the leader, who would parcel it out to the other boys.

"The parents, a lot of them, didn't want their boys to smoke or chew tobacco," says Ray. "I knew the mamas and papas would get on me. So I'd tell the boys, 'I'll give you'uns some smoking and chewing tobacco, but don't you tell your parents.'

"On the trip I bought a big plug that was not yet cut up to sell — Coon, Bull of the Woods, Apple, Bloodhound — one of them that was pressed into a wood

Triumph of the Omens

case, pressed in a machine and smelt good. I gave it to the biggest of the boys and told him to cut it up to share with the other'ns. Well, I went on, and heared noises. When I looked back they was a-fighting over the plug. The big'un was trying to keep it all. Gah, what a fight was a-going on. They got black eyes and bloody noses, and I thought for sure the parents would find what it was all about, and they'd come atter me. But they never did."

On his next visit to Sandy Flat, Ray brought a Barlow knife to divide the tobacco and candy himself. If there were too many to share his offering, he would distribute none. By now he had gained their confidences, and the boys felt it to their advantage not to harm the man who had been generous to them. Ray would admonish them not to fight. The boys would go home and tell their parents about "Mister Hicks, the good man who goes courting down at Sandy Flat," and in time a parent might see Ray and thank him for his handling of the restless boys.

Slow weeks passed, during which Ray was not sure he would "get started" with Rosa. But he visited often and sat by the warmth of the big fireplace; the family all played games and sang along with Ray.

"Gah, what good times."

Ray would care for the admiring Kell—toast marshmallows for him, play and sing his favorite hymns and ballads, swap yarns with him. But he did not yet know whether the still-shy Rosa would take him for her beau. Then, one afternoon before Ray was to come calling, the old man passed through the kitchen. He stopped before a seated Rosa, who today remembers that he shook a finger at her:

"If you don't sit with that boy when he comes, I'm a-gonna whop you with a hickory stick."

Rosa respected her grandfather, had always known him to be gentle, and knew that never before had he scolded her so. She began thinking that maybe she was wrong to be so standoffish, so rude. She went to her sisters and confided that she did not want to appear forward with her suitor, but perhaps indeed she had been too cool, too distant to a young man her whole family seemed to adore. Often, when Ray was visiting, Rosa would get up and go into the girls' bedroom to play the secondhand wind-up Victrola.

That evening, when Ray arrived, Rosa and a sister were seated by the hearth of the mudrock fireplace—a spot that was now a symbol for warmth and happy times. Four-foot logs were laid across the stone "andirons," and thrash beans were cooking in the pot. Ray had brought a sack of candy, enough for all the sisters; he "didn't want to shy any of them."

On impulse he sat down beside Rosa, and she did not move. The sister soon rose and left. The two were now alone, and no one else came into the room. They sat by the fire, and later Ray pulled the harmonica from his bib pocket and played a tune about a tragic love. He took notice of Rosa's new attitude; and he took notice, too, that they were left alone.

"That's the night when we got started."

Winter came on, and Ray made regular jaunts across Laurel Creek into the Sandy Flat country. Rosa was no longer shy. The two would sit in the parlor and play games, sing, and tell stories with the rest of the family. But at a certain hour, all would go to bed and leave Ray and Rosa alone. Rosa would put a single four-foot log on the fire when the family retired. Then Ray would stay well past the time the log was consumed. The stones held their heat long after the embers died. Many years later, Ray still savors the memory of the toasty hearth and the glow of cordiality from the Harmon family.

With a hundred and fifty dollars saved from his earnings at the sawmill, Ray brought a gray workhorse over in Beaverdam. He had many uses for it at the homeplace, and the horse would ease his workload. When his cousin Floyd came over in mid-December, Ray readily acceded to the idea of cutting and hauling wood for the Harmons. Floyd was already married into the family, and Ray hoped to be. They both knew the plight of the Harmons—that the wood they used for the old fireplace was split mostly by the girls, who used a well-worn crosscut saw to replenish a stack that was always low. The gray horse would enable Ray and Floyd to fell trees and drag them easily to the Harmons' home.

Ray had kept Rosa a secret. Even his family did not know he had been calling at the Harmon house. If word got out in his own neighborhood that he was courting a girl in Sandy Flat, Ray might be pestered by the "drinking boys." They might follow him there and "ruin it all."

On the day before he took the wood to the Harmons, he visited his grandmother Suzy Ann's store to buy Christmas candy for Rosa and Grandfather Kell.

There Suzy Ann told him that he had just missed Dory and her girl. She said they had just left, that Ray could catch them if he'd hurry.

Ray was amused. Dory and her shy girl from Beech Creek? The girl, Abby, who had run ahead of him on their long walk to the church gathering at Kell's house?

"That's all right," said a noncommittal Ray. He still had visions of the local boys getting drunk, following him, and finding out where he was courting. On the other hand, he did not want to mislead them so much that they would believe he was going to see Dory's shy daughter. He thought the best course was to keep quiet and to stay away from the Beech Creek girl.

"Suzy Ann told me, said, 'Ray, if you can get Dory's girl, you'd better be a-jumping. They ain't a better girl in the country than her. Course, I told them the same thing about you. They ain't a better boy than you.'"

Midwinter came, and Ray tramped through the snow to Sandy Flat. Most nights the temperature dropped far below freezing. At these times he did not walk all the way back to Old Mountain Road. Instead, he would slip into a barn and sleep in the hay.

"I learned about sleeping in the hay from my dogs. Never did build them no dog beds. They'd go dig in the haystacks.

"We'd be late coming in from a revival meeting down yander on Watauga River, so tired coming back over the mountains, and it up in the night. Some of us boys would just slip into a barn and lay there till daylight. We's just away and couldn't get home. Wore down."

In the cold January and February nights, Ray would roll up two light quilts before he visited Sandy Flat. He would leave the bundle on the sitting porch, or maybe in the Farthings' hayloft; on his late return he would stop off at the barn. He would pat down the hay to three inches thick and smooth out the lumps. One quilt he would lay over the hay pad and one over his body.

"I've laid in a barn with nothing but hay, but it's better with the quilts. Quilts don't let hayseeds get on you."

Even if others did not "cipher" it, the girl Abby and her mother, there on Beech Creek, were aware of Ray's pursuit of Rosa Harmon. They knew, too, that Rosa's mother, Mary Ellen, was "particular" and that she was protective of her daughters. Although Dory's young, blond daughter was shy, she wanted Ray to

Triumph of the Omens

come calling. The first step in getting him would be to drive him away from the Harmon house.

Soon the word went around: Ray Hicks drinks wine and whiskey. He is a wild man when he is "in the jug." In a drunken rage, he might even beat up Monroe, Rosa's father. Moreover, down at a little store in Rominger, Dory told Rosa's mother that if Rosa kept seeing Ray there might even be "a baby on the knee."

This did not seem plausible to Mary Ellen, but still she thought of Dory's gossipry and she brooded. How could a nice boy like Ray change faces so? How could he drink like that? He had been the most thoughtful person she knew. Could he be one fellow when single and another when married?

It was late February and the frozen mountains lay under snow. Ray made his way to Sandy Flat and warmed himself by the now-beloved mudrock fireplace. As usual, the first part of the evening was devoted to Kell, the grandfather. As Ray spun yarns with Kell, Rosa's mother came through the room occasionally. "Her eyes sparked every time she looked at me," says Ray. "I said to myself that something bad had gone wrong." But nothing was mentioned of the story that Ray was a drinker who might attack the father and "put a baby on the knee." Because he did not know of Dory's tale, Ray had no chance to deny it.

All that winter Ray spent more evenings in the Harmon house than he did at home. Now spring was coming. Though heavy snows fell in March, the weather between blizzards grew less wintry. Snowbirds flitted and the hoary mountains seemed to stir under their icy thatches. Soon the winds—blowing from Canada across the Great Lakes and through Kentucky and Tennessee— would bring spring fragrances. Groundhogs would scurry from their elaborate burrows; squirrels would chatter and crocuses would break through the moist, fecund soil. The mountain world would stir and shake off the ravages of winter. Happy sounds would bound off ancient rocks, and there would be beauty so awesome that even the most jaded and wearied would smile. The springs in all the years before would return to warm the bones and stir the blood.

From his grandfather, Ray borrowed a truck. He picked up Rosa at her home and drove her to Banner Elk, where they took a pre-marriage test. There would be a waiting period, and during that time Ray had things to do. Rosa's mother, whose eyes had "sparked" on Ray's visit in late February, had softened her demeanor. She was kinder, nicer. Still, Ray could not be sure that she felt the same about him as before. Once she told him that she wished just *one* boy would bother to ask for a daughter's hand; the others had all slipped off to marry in Mountain City, just across the Tennessee border.

When the betrothed couple returned from Banner Elk, Ray approached Rosa's father, who sat on the front porch. With him, Ray had the confidence born of familiarity. The exchange, he remembers, went something like this:

"Well, Monroe, you gonna let me take your girl, Rosa?"

"Yeah, Ray, I wouldn't know of no boy I'd rather take the girl than you. Perfectly all right."

Half the battle was over, and Ray asked where he could find the mother.

"She's out yander," said Monroe, pointing. "She's down there feeding the pigs."

Ray was aglow, but doubt still lurked. He remembered Mary Ellen's eyes that "sparked" during his visit the month before. He walked down the path and found her by the hog pen. She held the feed bucket and looked up at him. He still did not know about Dory's rumors and was puzzled when he recalled the mother's menacing glances. But today did he see a change? He spoke casually:

"You gonna let me take Rosa?"

The woman did not smile. Ray remembers that tears rose in her dark eyes. "She told me, said, 'Let me name a few things to you. I met Dory and her ashy-headed daughter at the store a few weeks back. She told me stories about you, about you drinking and fighting and maybe even putting a baby on the knee.' She wiped her eyes and then told me, 'I come within one of running you off.' "

Nevertheless, she had not taken Dory's word alone. She had visited her daughter Dorsey. She knew that both Dorsey and her husband, Floyd, knew Ray well. She told Dorsey of Dory's story, knowing her daughter would tell her truthfully the kind of husband Ray Hicks would be.

Dorsey quickly defended him. "She said, 'That's their tale. I know Ray. He ain't that kind. They don't even know him. It's just their way of getting you to run him off.' "

Rosa's mother told Ray that Dorsey saved him. "She told me, 'I came within the thump of my finger of running you off.'

"She said, 'Yeah, go marry Rosa.' "

It had been long years since Molly Lee told Ray he would have to wait for his bride. But when the last patches of snow melted in the north crevices, Ray Hicks and Rosa Harmon were married. Their only chivaree was a mild one when they returned that evening to Sandy Flat. Then Ray played his banjo and did a buck dance. He sang ballads that ranged over the history of his people—Scottish and English tunes that told of unrequited love. Here by the mudrock fireplace Ray Hicks sang triumphantly. When he played a hymn, they all joined in. Rosa at last had become his wife.

When the night was still young, he put Rosa's belongings into the bed of his grandfather's truck, then he took her to a tin-roofed cabin up the mountain and across from his mother's home. From here the newly marrieds could look down to the house in which Ray was born, could see beyond to the home of his grandparents, Benjamin and Julie, could scan the fields that Ray plowed. Every morning Rosa would go to the window and look out to the far mountains. She would plant dahlias and lupines that summer. Though she loved the little home she had grown up in back in Sandy Flat, the cabin here was her own, her nest, a refuge where she alone would be queen.

Ray had bought the place from his brother Lewis. He worked hard to pay for it and had long since retired the mortgage by the time he wedded Rosa.

In August he would be twenty-seven, and he had "seen it hard" much like the fabled Jack of his stories. Times would still be difficult, but now his bride, all of seventeen, would share his tasks and inspire him. No longer would he need to plod miles through the snow to see her, and no longer would he bear alone the weight of his mother's illnesses. Rosa would help tend to Rena, who also gathered new energy now that she had stopped "bairning" little ones.

Ray continued to bring cash into the little cabin by working at any job he could find. He hired himself out as a field laborer and a sawmill hand, but he continued to grow potatoes, cabbage, and corn in the plots around his cabin and in the fields around the homestead, too. At times he and his young wife would climb Beech Mountain, Dark Ridge, and Valle Mountain, taking large sacks to gather ginseng, bloodroot, galax, and black cohash. Ray's face and arms were bronzed, but Rosa shaded her creamy skin under a broad-brimmed hat. They worked happily together.

It was a bearable life, and because they had never known any better existence, they found beauty and comfort in small things. In contrast to the days when they lived in the homes of their parents, they were better off. They were young and strong and carried with them the love of their families. When the day's work was done, Ray might play his harmonica and banjo, and they would both sing. At times, Rosa would read aloud or Ray would recount Jack Tales and ghost stories.

To live well, they used all the wiles of their ancestors, who had inhabited this same rocky but picturesque land. To fill out their diets they picked "greens" from the mountain earth—wild plants called pokeweed, chicken galluses, spotted walker, branch lettuce, crow's foot, dandelion, yellow dock, plantain, and blackberry gar. They prepared the greens according to recipes given them by their mothers and grandmothers.

With gusto, Ray recalls the dishes his mother Rena prepared with branch lettuce: "Mom killed the wild taste by soaking it in hot buttermilk. Then she'd cut onions up in it, young top onions. Just cut the top and all, them onions with little heads. Heat it on the stove and kill it down to where it's kinda wilted. You talk about taste!"

Nearly all wild plants needed appetizing recipes, but a few were risky. Some, like pokeweed, required cautious treatment before they could be served. But Ray thinks pokeweed was good for one's health.

"Never did like the taste of it," says Ray, "but it was good for me. Rosa would mix it, parboil it, and then fry it in grease to kill the poison."

From between stalks of corn, creasies grew. Corn did not thrive well up the hillsides, but down along Laurel Creek, farmers might have fields of healthy corn, and there creasies sprouted abundantly.

On Beech Mountain's slopes—far up behind Ray and Rosa's cottage—there grew onionlike plants that Ray thought tasted better than a common onion. Mountain people called them "ramps," and they were normally fried. The flavor, Ray said, was like an onion, "except maybe better."

Other plants that could be found wild on Beech Mountain were good for care of the body. One could use plantain to draw out a splinter. When fat meat was not available, galax—heated to wilting and placed on a boil—would draw the corruption to a head.

"We call them 'wild,' but all plants started wild," says Ray. "We just started taming some of them. And a lot we learned from the Indians."

On summer evenings, between supper and dark, Ray and Rosa would sit on the porch of the cabin and sing the old songs. Because Rosa was his treasure, he wondered why so many love ballads were about men losing their women, even murdering them. Nearly all the people he knew mated for life; murders were nearly unheard of in his environment.

"I used to pull tobacco with a young feller over in Matney," Ray recalls. "Sometimes I'd play ballads for him, but when I'd sing about 'Omie Wise' and 'Pretty Polly,' he'd stop me . . . say he didn't want to hear no more murdering songs. They's a lot of killing in those songs.

"In the ballads, the boy might have such a feeling for the girl that he'd kill her afore he'd let the another'n have her. Says, 'If I can't have her, nobody else can.' But I've studied it, and I think they wasn't so many murders in the mountains. It's just that there's a lot of people and a lot of years gone by. And so these songs are sad and pretty, and people remember bad things better than good things. It might be that a lot of good things didn't make it through the years, but the bad ones got through. I still like to sing them old ones; and besides, lot of these songs got started in the old country."

So Ray would sing to Rosa, and at times they would sing together. Then, as though they had not talked of such things when they were courting, they would tell each other of their childhoods—the games they played, the songs they sang. They would laugh about how young ones do not recognize poverty, how they would sing and play even as their parents brooded. Though Rosa was happy with life in the little cabin, she still recalls delightedly the singing and playing of younger days:

"We would pick out the players—eenie, meenie, minie, moe—but we said other verses, too:

"Wire, bar, lumber, lock
Three geese in a flock
One flew east, one flew west,
One flew over the cuckoo's nest.

"And then there were the stories. The 'Old Man's Cold Hands' is one," says Rosa.

It was long, long ago, when the winter was really cold. There lived an old man and an old woman. They had to work. They lived so far from other houses they couldn't get people to come and gather wood. It was getting bad winter, and the old man had to go out in the cold each morning. He had to work all day to chop enough wood to do until morning. He said to his wife:

"Old woman, my hands get so cold. The wind blows so. My hands are about ready to come off."

And the woman had such a big feeling for him. Back then they didn't have no mittens, no gloves. Didn't even know how to make them.

When the woman was young, she used to make clothes, but she didn't know how to make mittens. So while she worked in the house during the day, she studied how she could do something to keep the old man's hands warm. And after supper she got her needles out, and her thread, and she studied. Late that night she sewed mittens with colored thread.

The next morning she gave the mittens to the old man, and he tried to put them on every way but he couldn't. There was no place for the thumbs. So, as usual, he left to cut wood with nothing covering his hands.

In the kitchen yard there was a dead bush, with rocks around the bottom of it. She took the mittens outside and hung them on a bush.

She studied again as she did her work. After the old man had gone to bed she got her needles out and worked on a different kind of mitten. When the old man tried them on in the morning, there was places for the thumb, but only three fingers. Again he left the mittens and went out into the cold. And again the old woman went into the kitchen yard and put the mittens on the dead tree. Now there were four funny little mittens hanging there—yellow and green—and they looked pretty, decorating the tree.

On the third day she did the same thing. After supper she got out her needles and thread. She worked and studied and twisted and had to think.

The next morning the old man tried on the mittens and they were good, but both for the right hand. He said, "Old lady, you try, but you don't seem to get nothing right." So she took the two little things and put them on the dead bush. Now there were six little things wiggling up there.

That evening she thought she had it figured out. "Now let's see," she said, "all I have to do is put a right hand with the left hand and they will mate."

Come morning. Great. She was pleased, and the old man was so tickled that he grabbed and kissed her. His hands stayed warm that day.

When spring came, that dead bush began to put out little green buds. "Oh," said the woman. "I thought the tree was dead, but it's putting out leaves." And she kept watching the plant.

A sassafras tree!

Triumph of the Omens

At the story's end, Rosa exclaims: "Look at the leaves on a sassafras tree. See all those little mittens. They come one for one hand, one for the other—more for the right hand than the left.

"That's why they call a sassafras tree a mitten bush."

Back at Sandy Flat, Monroe Harmon talked with Ray. He knew his son-in-law was handy with a saw and hammer. He told Ray that his remaining daughters wanted more room, and that he wanted to take out the mudrock chimney to make room for an addition.

Ray wanted to help, but he had always hoped that the fireplace would never be destroyed. Yet in the spring of the year, he acceded to Monroe's wishes and set about tearing off the sides of the house to enlarge it. The chimney would have to be eliminated because it occupied so much room. But Ray could not bring himself to help tear it down.

"It drawed and could burn logs up to five feet long," Ray says. "Atter the stones got really hot the fire would keep all that little house warm. Even atter the fire was out it would keep you warm for another hour or two. And you could lay a green piece of wood on that and it'd burn like oil."

When the house was completed, two new rooms made the girls happy. But when Ray looked at the finished work he tried to remember the house before it was changed:

"I can see it in my mind. See the old chimney. The way it was before they tore it down. That's the reason I can tell stories. I can see that little old rough house she was raised in. And what fine people they was. Lived hard. Honest and humble people. Her dad's word was just as good as his own paper.

"Me'n Rosa would set there and talk about how things would be atter we was married. And it was better, the way we seed it. Now the mudrock fireplace is gone, right where we set. I keep it in my mind. It's not there no more.

"But Rosa and me's still with each other."

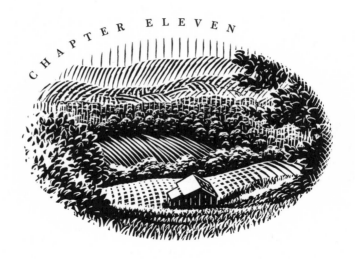

CHAPTER ELEVEN

Below the Rock of Lost Gold

Besides tending her vegetable garden, Rosa raised foxglove, black-eyed susans, rebeccas, and lilies of the valley. Ray worked at "mechanicking" and in his potato and cabbage fields. Together they looked after his mother, who lived down the hill at the homeplace.

Above them and to the west rose one of the many prominences of Beech Mountain; to look at, it was much the same as any other granite outcropping, but its oft-told legend set it apart.

The story goes that two strangers from afar were guided up the rocky slopes by an Indian who pointed out glittering metal in the stone crevices. When the men were satisfied they had found a gold vein amid the rocks, they expressed their gratitude to the Indian. With picks and axes they labored for many days digging out small gold nuggets. At last they believed they had exhausted the vein and began to break camp.

Loading their cache on the back of a donkey, they made their way down the north side of the summit. Somewhere along the slope, the donkey stepped into a crevice and broke its leg. Without a beast of burden, the men reasoned, they could carry a small load of gold but would need to leave the bulk of it behind. They shot the donkey and, with the help of their guide, buried the treasure near the fallen animal. As they worked with pick and shovel, the men talked. One told the other that, now the gold had been taken from the granite, he did not trust the Indian. When they came back for it later, he said, the gold might be gone.

Near dusk, one of the prospectors shot the red man and left him for dead; but when the dawn came, as the two prepared their knapsacks to depart, they discovered the Indian had stolen away, leaving a trail of blood that faded west into the mountain forest.

The men drew a map, then climbed the rocky promontory and spent days carving a code, R-A-X, into the stone. The letters, which could be seen from several points of the valley, were intended to help them when they returned. Now they moved the heaviest load of gold from its place beside the donkey, thinking that should the Indian return he would not be able to locate the treasure.

The Indian did come back one day, and he told the story to pioneers who had built log cabins along Beech Creek. With the settlers, the red man searched for months but could never locate the treasure. Back in his own village, he marveled how two men could have cut such large letters on the mountain's face.

It is said that one of the white men came back alone but could not find the hidden gold; the other fortune-hunter had died.

The legend fascinated Ray's father; he and Ray would often climb the peak and dig around the site in search of the treasure.

At times even today, when the sun slants at certain angles, the curious letters stand out. As a young man, Nathan would trim trees and shrubbery that grew beneath the letters. From the front porch of his home, he liked to point out to visitors the mysterious carving. Oddly, though, when one climbed the rock to try to see the letters close up, there would appear to be nothing there but a growth of rock moss.

"I've been up there and pulled off the moss," says Ray. Beneath the growth he could see only rock that seemed chiseled without form. Yet, from down the hill, the letters show crisply in the sun's cross light.

"There never was any doubt with the old people," says Ray. "They knew gold was up there somewhere. Right off that R-A-X."

A Cherokee who lives near Old Fort says that Indians were almost gone from the Watauga country when white settlers began to come in. But there remains in

Below the Rock of Lost Gold

these hills a great respect for the Native Americans. Some pioneers in the area married Indians, and today their descendants proudly claim the heritage.

"There's Indian blood in me," says Ray. "And I've had friends that were more Indian than I was.

"We all learned from the Indians. Grandfather Benjamin said most of what he knew about living in this rough country was handed down by Indian people."

"My best buddy was half Indian, and, gah, he knew how to live in the wild. We killed small game and gathered herbs together; sometimes we'd go out and spend the night up on the mountain. I always felt safe being out like that and him knowing all he knew about the wilderness."

In the lull of one summer, when there was no call for farm work, Ray and his friend took cutting tools and two large sacks and climbed Beech Mountain. They peeled black cherry bark, which the next day they would carry to market. Once they had penetrated the deep woods of Pinnacle Ridge, they found only flickerings of sunlight sifting through the leaves; they were astonished when night dropped upon them.

"It got dungeon dark," says Ray. "We felt around there a-trying to find our own way out. We knew we wasn't lost, but if we tried to feel our way down that canyon we'd get a leg broke, or maybe find ourselves down at Banner Elk, so far from home."

At last the two made their way to a clearing, a place called Ponds Field, in recognition of a pioneer who once had owned the land and grazed cows there. The field was made up of thirty or forty acres of level land atop one of the highest places on the great mountain. Here the friend told Ray to stand and wait. In the pitch dark he would try to find a tree that would give him the easiest and safest direction to go down the mountain.

"Talk about dark," says Ray, closing his eyes and stretching his hands out front. "You couldn't see nothing. Dark and foggy. And so my friend's gone and left me standing there. In about twenty minutes he came back. I heared him coming in the racket of the leaves. Then he got up to me, he said he thought he had found the right tree."

Now Ray gets up from the old glider on his porch. He steps off to the ground and goes to the large ash tree where the old troubadours once played for the New York ballad collectors; he points to the tree's base.

"See, my friend showed me that if you've got the right tree, like this one is, you can find west easy. At the bottom it's a little rounder, and there'll be a little bit of moss. On the north side where the timber has been frozen by icy winds it's rougher and there's even more moss on it. Now on the southeast side where the sun hits, there's less scale and no moss."

After they read their bearings, "just like a compass," Ray and his companion felt their way to an old wagon trail; from there they groped their way along the ruts to Ray's home.

"The right tree won't be in the sheltered valley," he says. "Can't find your way by hugging it. It won't be frozen on one side, but the whole tree will be pretty smooth. You need to get on a ridge where the timber freezes. There won't be much growth on the north side, but the two warm sides will grow fast, and the heart of the tree will always be to one side."

He goes now to the stump of another tree and shows how the rings on the north side are narrower and the heart is skewed to that bearing. He traces points with his finger.

"I've seen tree stumps with cracks going all four ways of the compass, but for hugging a live tree to get directions you've got to find it on a frozen mountain-top, up high, like the one my buddy found. There we was over a mile up when he found that tree. Right here at this ash tree, it's forty-two hundred feet. Here where me'n Rosa live."

On the slopes and in the valleys of the Beech, settlers would hunt small game when farm work did not require their time, or they would haul tanbark, or look for nuts, or dig for herbs. If they had to name an effort that yielded the most spending money, it would be herb gathering. Domestic crops normally were grown merely to fill home needs. Indeed, most of the land upon which they hunted for herbs was owned by large companies or wealthy individuals, and on this land they could find exotic ginseng and hundreds of medicinal herbs.

On many mornings in season, Ray and Rosa would take large sacks and go up into herb-laden forests. If they had a good day they might come back before nightfall but, if gathering the plants took longer, they would spend the night among the trees and the sounds of wild birds and animals. As their children grew, Ray and Rosa would take them into the forests and teach them to know by sight all the roots and herbs; they showed them how to remove plants from the woods without mutilating the source.

Some landowners refused permission for outsiders to come onto their property, says Ray. "If you're up agin it, some had rather see you dead as to let you get any herbs off their land."

Lumber and mining companies owned vast properties, and they usually would permit local inhabitants to pull, dig, and peel roots, herbs, and bark — even to cut selected trees, though they warned that no timber should be cut that might later be used for carpenter lumber. They encouraged the cutting of black cherry and beech trees for firewood, for profitable, lumber-producing trees might grow back in place of the felled ones. They also invited the residents to cut crooked trees — water oak, hemlock, white pine, and basswood — that were marked by painted gashes on the bark. Only straight timber could be used for milling.

Inevitably, the granted liberties were abused. When this happened, signs would show up at a property's edge to warn against trespassing.

"People don't know how to live," says Ray. "The thoughtless ones ruin it for the rest of us."

As time passed, the landowning companies became less lenient. They were taking more and more products from their own forests, and in doing so they discovered more violations, many unintentional. People who gathered herbs and hunted in the Beech wilderness shied away from certain properties even when they had permission to be there. They simply did not want to share the blame for breaking the rules.

Herbs were widely used in medicine, and the Watauga and Avery County hills were an important source for doctors and patients. Many kinds of medicines were made from the mountains' bounty. Herb gatherers would take plants and bark to Valle Crucis or Boone or Lenoir to sell. Besides providing cash, herbs were also the basis of home remedies. Medicines in the hills were almost totally derived from plants, roots, and barks. The local traveling "doctors" would prescribe nothing but herbal remedies.

The herb that brought the most cash year after year was ginseng, a sweet-smelling root that was both tasty and had a variety of uses. Its chief value, however, lay in its mythical properties as an aphrodisiac; the overwhelming bulk of it eventually reached China. Fifty years ago ginseng was widely used; today it is not easy to find, though it remains a source of cash for some hill people like Ray's son Ted. In Ray's younger days, ginseng was gathered at the north wing of Beech Mountain, where buckeye trees grow thickly and where, today, second-home developments have all but destroyed the beds. Now, by law, there is a starting time for picking ginseng; the plant's berries must reach a mature state before root gathering is permitted.

Another useful plant was spikenard for the kidneys, says Ray. He rattles off names of other herbs and their cures: "Yellow dock that the Indians called yellow root for your stomach; gelico, that they call angelica anymore . . . to purify your blood; wild cherry bark for coughs, for your stomach, too; and sassafras bark, that people still make for tea, and nearly everybody knows it's a good spring tonic."

Wild plants were used for more than medicines. Tanbark was stripped from trees and taken to Bristol as a tanning agent; log moss was pulled from dead and rotting wood and sold as mats at funerals; galax leaves provided durable greenery for florists.

Especially in those early days with Rosa—when he had not yet begun to work on old cars—Ray gathered log moss and tanbark. He bought an old truck, repaired it, and carried his harvest to market beyond Roan Mountain.

Ray always hauled out the mature growth of moss from the forests. Few other inhabitants gathered moss because it was heavy, difficult to carry out of the deep woods, and required a wagon or truck to take it to market. But it was a resource Ray found easy to harvest now that he could carry loads to his truck at the forest's edge. As he gathered the moss, he would bundle it and leave it at stops along the way.

In the woods one morning, above the Watauga River, he came across an abundance of log moss within a narrow band where lightning or blight had once felled great trees. The forest was otherwise thick with vegetation, and log moss grew near the edge of the trees. Ray planned to bind the loads, leave them in piles along the paths where he gathered them, and then carry one bundle at a time to his truck. He saw a field and thought if he could park his truck at its edge, he could save time. A farmhouse stood close by, near a spring, and Ray hallooed until the owner came out. The man gave Ray permission to cross the field, but he pointed to the sky:

"You'll need to make haste; looks like we're in for a cloudburst."

Ray went back into the forest and had shouldered out two loads when he heard distant thunder. He hurried now, calling upon his body to give him the strength to haul out the remainder of his log moss. As he went into the forest for the third time he saw a misty fall of rain upstream, and he gauged it to be "one of those river storms," a safe distance away. He was well into the interior when the storm seemed to throw its fury directly at him. Thunder clapped simultaneously with the lightning that slammed into the denseness of the mountain jungle all around.

Ray decided to wait out the river storm because, in his experience, such tempests came on strong and left quickly. He sat beneath a canopy of low trees until, sure enough, the downpour slackened and its pelting of the leaves softened to a pattering. But as he started to come out, he was blinded in a millisecond of blue light when a firebolt struck so close that its incredible sound seemed to come out of its white flash.

As he lay on the soaked leaves and smelled the burnt air, he saw that a giant oak standing twenty feet away had been shorn of its bark; a pale spiral strip ran the length of its trunk to its roots.

A moment later, he thought he caught the movement of something in the fog, a jerky motion amid the twisting trees and limbs. The figure seemed to crumple behind a chestnut log. A wildcat? Maybe even a mountain lion.

Wind, rain, and deafening noises swept through the forest, and Ray looked about for any harbor that would shelter him from lightning strikes. At last he made out the form of twin chestnut trees that had been yanked up by their roots, perhaps even as long ago as the 1940 flood.

Sometimes in the mountains long periods of rain renders the soil soft and porous, so that the gusts that follow soaking rains can easily topple great trees, even those that are dead and have no leaves to catch the wind. The roots of such fallen trees break out of the ground and jut above their crater. Ray saw such a hole beneath a downed chestnut tree and ran to it, crawled in, and waited. Looking out from his sheltered haven, he watched the place where he thought he had seen something moving in the storm, but nothing seemed to be there.

Then a strange thing happened: Balls of lightning rolled swiftly over dead chestnut limbs, over his feet, along the forest floor.

"It kinda looked like fire, and it didn't strike or make noise. Just rolled like a fireball. Somebody told me a while back what that kind of lightning is called, but I don't remember. I just know I don't want to see it again."

Presently the storm slackened, and when Ray pulled himself from the crater he again saw movement across the forest floor. Through the damp haze, he thought he saw an eerie, upright figure slowly creeping out of a clutch of hemlocks. Closer it came until at last he could make out a tall and bearded man, drenched and bewildered. The man seemed to be carrying two large milk pails.

"He yelled at me," Ray recalls. "He came a-running, and I seed then it was somebody I knowed. Ephraim Creed, older'n me.

"I asked him what he was doing there, and then I could see that he had been collecting lizards to sell. People would do that. Sell it for fishing bait.

"Ephraim asked me to help him. Said his girl needed cash bad, and he was trying to rumble up a little money for her.

"I told him I'd help but that I had to get my log moss out of there. In this country it can turn clear and in thirty minutes it'll go boom, boom, boom."

But Ray deferred his own chores, because his older friend looked like a "drowned possum" and seemed to need the money so badly. They set out to find lizards—Ray to the top of the mountain and Ephraim down by the creek. Within thirty minutes, thunder announced the coming of another storm. Ray had more than half-filled his bucket in lizards, and as he ran for shelter, he cradled the bucket carefully. He hurriedly picked up fragments of a fallen chestnut tree, put them together like a tent, and, holding his lizard bucket, started to duck into his makeshift shelter.

"But lightning hit the bucket and jerked it out of my hand," he says, "causing me to lose two or three dozen lizards."

His hair stood on end and his ears rang from the strike, and he ran—he knew not why—across the clearing to a towering locust tree. Grandfather Benjamin had often told him that a locust tree drew lightning, but in Ray's sudden fear he thought only of shelter.

As he came to rest there, partly protected from the rain, he made out the form of his friend running "humped over and carrying his lizard bucket." Ephraim glimpsed the crude wood tent Ray had thrown up and did not hear Ray call as he dashed directly to the shelter. He had barely set down his bucket when lightning struck. Fire lighted the bucket, and the fringe of the bolt knocked Ephraim down. In a moment he staggered to his feet, grabbed the bucket, and ran off the peak in the direction of Banner Elk.

When the storm diminished, Ray picked up his own bucket and went in search of his friend. Soon he found him inside a sheltering rock, nursing minor wounds and much shaken from the glancing lightning strike. They walked back to the clearing where Ray had left his truck, with Ephraim tightly holding his crumpled bucket of lizards. He had not noticed that the creatures had been electrocuted.

Below the Rock of Lost Gold

When the Scots, English, and Germans settled the mountains of Watauga, they survived by helping each other; randomly, they also learned from friendly Indians. By reckless adventuring they managed. Advice on herbal remedies, snakebite wounds, crop planting, hog slaughtering—all constituted words to live by. Whether founded upon fact or superstition, counsel from elders was rarely questioned.

Grandfather Benjamin had told Ray never to shelter under a locust tree. This might or might not have been informed advice, but there were no statistics to confirm or deny its truth. Such beliefs were comforting. Besides, grandparents knew! They had lived a long time and were nearer to the source of the Holy Bible and the nebulous past.

While Ray was still young, Benjamin shared his wisdom. A dutiful, respectful Ray absorbed it all.

"Now, son, when you're out and a thunderstorm comes, don't never shelter under a locust. Careful of a dead locust, especially. A dead'un will draw lightning. But now a green locust will pull lightning pretty bad, too. If you're ever caught out like that, get under a beech tree . . . like the ones across Pinnacle Ridge. Any beech will do. Rugged. Old. If you live long enough, you'll never see many beech trees that's been hit by lightning."

"Sure enough," says Ray. "I've got my first beech tree to see struck, but I've seen lots of hemlocks and pine trees hit . . . lots of them."

If Ray had a choice, though, he'd find a sheltering rock:

"Yiah, that's where the Indian people stayed when they was on the river in the summertime. I know of some rock shelters where a man could take lumber and fill it in and make him a good house. Build him a flue on the outer edge. Yiah. Be two rooms in it. Well, you could make four rooms in some. Partition it off, you could. They's some back yander . . . two families . . . that just stayed under a rock. Some of them walled in their sheltering-rock houses with mud or rock or oak. Like log houses. Yiah, they's a lot that way.

"Down here on the Watauga River, they's two rocks there where white men cured their tobacco just like the Indians did. They kept bale hay there under it, too. Later some kept tractors and farm equipment under it. On the Watauga. Yiah, they hung a big tobacco crop under this one. That rock gets hot and cures out the prettiest tobacco. Dries out with the sun heating the rock. They cured their hay under that rock. Let the wind stir through it. They's one rock down there we was under, I guess a hundred Indian people stayed there at one time. Watauga River. Down there where the Indians left those arrow-heads."

When he was not working, Ray's favorite place as a young boy was a shelter-ing rock on the river. "Seemed like magic there," he says. "I thought I could hear voices. It was like they teached me . . . that this was God a-talking, not our language, but his own creation. I got scared. When I was young I was scared of God. And I'd get under them rocks, it a-raining and water running off the rock. And I'd listen . . . seems like I could nearly understand the words of God. And directly I'd go out from under the rock and get wet and freeze. Mama would al-ways tell me, said, 'Ray, someday you'll want to talk to God.' But I was scared of God . . . feared he might tell me something that's a bad thing.

"But finally I got under the rock and called it what it was, that voice of God. But then I found out. What it was, really, was a little thin rock that had been froze every since this planet's been here. It froze and so much gravel and sand got in it. The little thin places would make this sound when drips of water would hit it. And it would rattle and make talking sounds: Whrup. Whrup. Whrup.

"Then the soft wind in there would make sounds, too, sounds that would scare a little boy. It was like a seashell. I've listened to the seashells that people brought to the mountains. I could put a seashell to my ear. What I heard, they said, was the sea a-roaring. Gah, it makes a roar, you know. Well, the sheltering rocks do that. It ain't the sea, but the air goes in that cave and the wind whistles and rolls around in there. The sheltering rock was a lot like that. To a scared lit-tle boy, it sounded like God a-talking. Whrup. Whrup. Whrup."

Ray and Rosa's first babies were born in the snuggery below the Rock of Lost Gold. Those early days were filled with normal farm chores and with child-caring; but each parent also worked to help Ray's oft-bedridden and widowed mother, Rena, who had two children of her own still at home, neither old enough to support themselves.

Although he now lived up the hill and away from the homestead, Ray re-mained the rock upon which Rena anchored her wishes, and now she counted on him all the more for sustenance. Often her whole income was a small welfare check that covered young Jack so long as he remained in school. In times when she felt well, she hooked rugs, and others sold them for her. But in the main, Rena Hicks's life seemed continually beset with woes.

Below the Rock of Lost Gold

Yet for Ray, tending his mother seemed less onerous than before; Rosa now shared the tasks, and both she and Ray adored the gentle and pious Rena.

Ray liked to sit on the small porch of his little cabin and look upon the old homeplace just below. He could see the big barn to the right, the springhouse and sheds in front. Beyond were trees and fields and the house of his departed grandparents, beloved Benjamin and Julie. Often he mused on the past, seeing the small boy Ray walking from the old house to his grandparents' where he learned the old stories.

The low ridge on the other side of Benjamin and Julie's old home marked the beginning of Oliver Hollow, which leveled off at Laurel Creek. Beyond, the forested terrain edged upward to Long Ridge, then down across Watauga River and up Tester Mountain. Farther distant were sweeping and undulating summits that screened the dawning sun and made the day shorter: Rich Bald, Snake, Elk Knob, Sugar Tree, and the mountains of Tennessee and Virginia. These marked the northern and eastern boundaries of Ray's existence. He felt that somewhere beyond these great misty rims lay opportunity, but he was sure he would never venture beyond them.

Already in his hearty youth he wore the scars and infirmities of a thorny life. Nearly a decade before, he had seen other young farmers go off to war, but he could not be among them. Yet somehow, he was amply fit for the scrabbly existence of the backwoods. Besides, he often pondered, a higher power might be protecting his life so he could glorify and preserve the ways of his passing elders.

November 18, 1949, was a cold, lifeless day on Old Mountain Road. Rena stirred in the house, preparing to visit her seriously ill father. Ray, in his seventeen-year-old Chevrolet pickup, would drive his mother to the house of his grandparents Andrew Jackson and Suzy Ann Hicks. There he expected to remain the whole morning, because Rena would need a lot of time to bolster her father, to comfort her mother.

Here, in the cleanly kept house where the schoolboy Ray once stopped off to spend the night in the blizzard, where his grandfather told him that the potato bug could be wiped out if people would fight it, the adult Ray now sat in silence by the firelight. He faced the west window and looked toward the little store where he had bought licorice and marshmallows to take to young Rosa Harmon's home.

Grandfather Andy lay sleeping under a mound of quilts in the same room. From time to time he would groan, and Suzy Ann would look anxiously toward her daughter. Rena tried to speak comforting words, but she thought her father seemed to have faded since her last visit two days before.

As mother and daughter spoke in subdued tones, something thumped heavily at the east window. Ray heard the noise but did not see its source.

Suddenly he saw alarm in his mother's face; she had been facing the window and had seen the impact. "I thought her face turned pale," says Ray, "but she told us it was probably a bird. Sometimes birds don't see windows when they fly, specially on gray days like that one."

A few minutes later there was a splintering crash, the sound this time coming from the west window; glass shattered into small pieces, much of it falling into the room. Suzy Ann clasped her hands to her mouth. "She wanted to scream," said Ray, "But she didn't. Didn't want to wake up Grandpa." Old Andy stirred briefly, but without opening his eyes.

Now a fidgeting Suzy Ann asked Ray if it was a bird, and he told her he thought it was.

Rena, overwrought, arose from her chair and left the room. In moments she returned, still shaken, with a sedge broom in hand. As she swept glass fragments onto a folded paper, her voice trembled.

"She told me to get something to stop up the hole in the window. She didn't want the air a-blowing in on Grandpa."

Before long Ray had found material to cover the window, then he told his mother that they must be going. Both promised Suzy Ann they'd return the next day.

In the truck, the still-pale Rena asked her son if it was a dove that hit the west window.

"Mama," he said, "it wasn't like any dove I've seed. It was a dove all right, but it was white." He told her it was "whiter than bleached flour, the brightest thing I ever seed. Nearly put my eyes out."

Ray says his mother told him: "What we both seed, Ray, was the Holy Ghost Dove."

Ray recalls he had once heard of the Holy Ghost Dove, of how sometimes it came and made its sign three days before a death.

"I said, 'You sure, Mama?'"

"She said, 'I *seed* it son, seed it the first time it hit the window, seed your

Below the Rock of Lost Gold

grandpa's body heave up. Then, when it broke the other window, I knew it was the Holy Ghost Dove. But, Ray, I couldn't tell Mama that in three days Dad would go to meet his Maker.' "

On November 21, Andrew Jackson Hicks died.

Thirty months later, on a fair Sunday morning in August, young Jack and a cousin left Rena's home to go to church. Around noon Rena's brother Ben knocked on her door. He told her that Jack had not gone to church, as he had told her. Instead, Jack and Ben's son had joined the bigger boys down at Laurel Creek, and Jack had drowned.

Jack had wanted to learn to swim, to surprise his mother, but in the mountains swimming was a rare sport, not usually counted among the skills of young men thereabouts. Warm seasons were naturally brief, and there were few streams deep or placid enough for bathers to enjoy. But in the cold waters of Laurel Creek, the 1940 flood had carved a deep hole. Here, only a few strong swimmers were able to brave the swift undertow. Jack, trying to paddle through water he could otherwise have stood erect in, drifted into the whirlpool and became panicked in its depths. His cousin said the boy strangled and thrashed and quickly was sucked beneath the surface. His body was found snagged on an underwater ledge.

Already Rena's lantern had grown dimmer. The long-past deaths of three infant children and the more recent losses — first her husband and then her father — challenged both her faith and her lamblike meekness. She had seemed composed. But now, Jack.

Jack was the last of Rena's brood of thirteen, the first to die beyond infancy. All but her youngest daughter, soon to leave, were now gone from the homeplace. Even though Ray and Rosa lived up the hill and came to see her daily, the old dwelling felt empty and cavernous.

Rena had begun to depend on Jack, the schoolboy, as a man of the house, the Ray of latter days. News of his death crumpled her as had no other thing.

There was no choice now: Ray and Rosa would have to close their honeymoon cottage and move into the big house. In many ways it would be better for all, but to Rena the noise of Ray and Rosa's small children also signaled her loss of control over a home she had lived in for most of her life. She felt a strangeness, an uncertainty. Her middle-aged years would be meaningless, at least in her own reckoning.

But Ray and Rosa were hearty and zestful. They would bring up their brood there. From the orchard they would harvest apples; from the fields they would glean potatoes, cabbages, corn, and beans. Ray would find odd jobs; he would "mechanick" and help build houses in Boone or labor in someone else's fields. In the fall, the vivacious Rosa would dry apples and corn and beans. She would line preserved foods along the sawdust-packed walls of a nearby shed. Together, Rosa and Ray would take the oldest of their children onto the Beech to help gather galax and herbs. Before the snows came they would go through the garden, cut the stems and bury cabbages upside down in their places. Then, through the winter, the still-crisp cabbages would be brought in as needed to be cooked or eaten raw.

Rena never stopped missing her Nathan, even though the pressure of dealing with his mercurial acts and ceaseless ambitions had taken a toll on her health. Nonetheless, from Jack's drowning until her own death fifteen years later, Rena lived better than she had since she was first married at the age of thirteen.

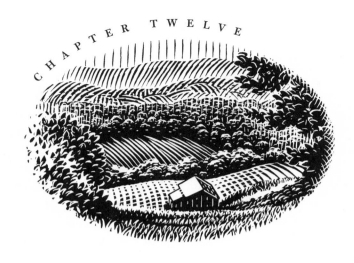

CHAPTER TWELVE

The Passing of the Torch

To any visitor from off the mountain, the day would seem pleasant and mild. To Ray Hicks's aunt, Nettie Hicks Presnell, and her dulcimer-making husband Edd, any day is hot that sees the thermometer break eighty. This is such a day.

Nettie sits on the stoop of the small workshop while Edd works inside. Noises from his tools at times interclude her soft words. She is the baby sister of long-dead Nathan Hicks, the last living offspring of Benjamin and Julie, who tended their brood here on this very site at the end of Old Mountain Road. Several hundred yards up the road is the house her father helped her brother Nathan build seventy-seven years earlier. It is the place where Ray Hicks grew up, and where he still lives today.

Nettie walks with difficulty; she is frail and feeble, but her blue eyes glitter. Inside Edd's shop an electric saw hums. Outside, Nettie talks of the days when she played Edd's dulcimers. In those times, recording company people came and visitors were always dropping by. She played "Shady Grove" and "Amazing Grace" and many other tunes that echoed the far-off drone of bagpipes. She is overly modest: "Anybody that can sing a tune can play a dulcimer."

Soon the woodwork noises cease and Edd emerges. He is smallish and walks quickly in a way that belies his age; his beard falls to the waist and his eyes flash slate-blue. Obviously he is an energetic and impatient person. His first attention is given to Nettie, whom he eases from the cane-bottomed chair. Nettie grasps her walker and is guided by Edd; she moves with small, shuffling steps across the yard.

Compared to his neighbors, Edd Presnell has prospered. He and Nettie lived in Benjamin and Julie's old homeplace until he built a brick ranch home on the opposite knoll. He did well as a farmer, applying all his knowledge of modern agriculture. At his leisure he made and sold dulcimers, but soon his name got around, and more and more people came to buy his instruments. Also he and Nettie fashioned animals and birds from wood. They shared their knowledge with their son, Baxter, who with his wife Reva made a thriving business of it. All the Presnells—Edd, Nettie, Baxter, and Reva—sell their crafts at fairs. They have gone as far afield as California to show their wares, and they are admired around Beech Mountain as people who have made the most of their heritage.

The Presnells work hard, and there is a demand for their handicrafts, but to earn a good living they must make many instruments and carve the likenesses of many wild creatures. It is a slow and careful process, and every minute of daylight is valued; little time is wasted from Monday through Saturday.

But this morning Edd Presnell will stop his work for an hour or so. The son of Nettie's niece is coming for a visit. Frank Proffitt Jr. is expected to drive over from his Pottertown home that is snug in the valley between Elk Knob and Snake Mountain. These are distinctive peaks that can be seen in the misty distance from Edd and Nettie's place. Frank Junior will drive across the Tennessee line at Trade and angle back into North Carolina.

In the back seat of his Ford sedan, Frank Junior has nestled a banjo and dulcimer. At the Presnell place he will ask Edd once again about instrument crafting. He never seems to tire of listening, and he knows the articulate Edd will enjoy time out from his work.

Ray and Rosa are expecting their nephew for lunch, but his first stop will be at his granduncle's place at the dead end of Old Mountain Road. He arrives in early morning, and Edd is already at work, sanding wood for dulcimers.

Grinning through his beard, Edd greets Frank Junior and tells him that he is feeling old, that his feet hurt, and that it is no wonder. He says he was born in 1916 and "didn't have a pair of storebought shoes until I was five." The men laugh, and Edd begins telling Frank Junior things he knows his visitor wants to hear:

The Passing of the Torch

"Franklin," he says, using the name he called his grand-nephew years before, "if people hadn't lived on the farm there would have been no way to make a living, but I don't know; maybe it was better back then."

He says his family had enough to eat, that they did not have good clothes but took care of what they had.

"You take the young people now; they're wearing clothes out in public that I'd be ashamed to wear even at home where nobody could see me. Over in Virginia a couple Saturdays ago, I saw a boy with his jeans threadbare all up and down. Air conditioned. Past decency. I thought about it: It's style to them, but when I was a lad I didn't have a choice. I wore mine like that because I didn't have no others to wear."

Edd recalls that despite the lack of warm clothing, children went to school no matter how cold the weather. Only high water kept them away.

"If it was cold you went; if it was raining you went; if it was snowing you went. I attended for four or five years without missing a day.

"We learned! Had good teachers; but it's different now. Teachers can't do nothing with students. There's even a law that kids can't be punished no matter what they do. Over here at Cove Creek a year ago, one told her teacher, 'I just dare you to spank me.'"

Edd remembers that the first dulcimer he ever heard (he does not say "delcimore" in the way of most people hereabout) was one his sweetheart Nettie played.

"I was fifteen or sixteen, and Nettie brought the dulcimer over and played it. She wasn't bashful about playing."

It was an instrument Nettie's father Benjamin made, and when Edd was nineteen he patterned his first dulcimer from this one. It was hourglass-shaped and had heart holes on its face.

"Hearts denote happiness," says Edd, "and pine trees, sorrow."

He says that when a boy made a dulcimer for his girlfriend, he would put hearts on the dulcimer's body. If the lovers broke up, the boy would make another dulcimer and carve pine trees on it.

"One woman wanted an axe carved in her mountain harp. She said an axe meant a lot to her. I never asked why."

Edd sold his first homemade dulcimer to Nathan for a wholesale price of three dollars. That was around the time when Nathan first started shipping banjos and, upon Frank Warner's advice, sold them for five dollars. Edd made several more for Nathan but also sold a few outside.

"The way you made one then, not polished and all, it would take three days and you'd take plenty of time on it. You'd not sand it . . . you'd dress it with a hand plane to take off splinters. Didn't have over thirty hours in it. When I sold one to Nathan, the three dollars I'd get would give me about ten cents an hour, and that was pretty good."

Frank Junior, whose father's version of the Tom Dooley ballad helped set off the craze for folk music, listens hungrily. He asks about fret wire, the metal strips normally fitted along the necks of most stringed instruments to mark the notes.

"For years, we used broom wire," says Edd. "I've tore up many a good broom when wire wasn't rusted yet. Used that for years. Homer Ledford up in Kentucky used broom wire until he started getting new wire from a factory there at Berea College."

Edd doesn't remember exactly when he began using wire made specifically for frets—probably at the time that the demand for dulcimers heightened, during the folk-revival mania of the sixties.

"When I first started, there wasn't much market for them. Then along about that time I remember I had orders for seventy dulcimers at one time. Everybody wanted them for Christmas, and this was in September or October. Somebody had to wait."

The folk music fad launched Edd's business; he began showing his dulcimers at the State Fair.

"Kept going to Raleigh for five years before I sold a dulcimer there," he says. "That was several decades ago and thirty-five dollars was a price that scared people away."

Years later, one night in Raleigh, he dreamed a man came to him and said he wanted a dulcimer. In the dream the man handed Edd a fifty-dollar bill, a silver dollar, and a half-dollar.

The next day a man came in, inspected a dulcimer, and said he'd take it.

"He gave me a fifty-dollar bill, a dollar bill, and a half-dollar. Just like in the dream, except the dollar was not silver. Some people say dreams don't come true, but all I needed to make this one come true was a silver dollar instead of the dollar bill."

The Passing of the Torch

Until the sun climbs to the top of the sky, Frank Junior stays asking questions of the old craftsman. He wants to know the kinds of wood used in dulcimers, how wood is bent, how wood is dried.

Edd's answers reveal that he learned much from Frank Junior's grandfather, Nathan Hicks, more than a half-century ago.

"Nathan made dulcimers the old way. He'd use poplar for the back and front and wahoo [winged elm] for the sides," says Edd. "He'd go into the woods and find a wahoo—green and about two inches through. He'd split it open and cut the heart out of it. Wahoo was good for bending; get it green and it'd bend easy."

Edd tells Frank Junior that he doesn't like to work with kiln-dried wood, that it takes twelve months of air-drying for every inch of the lumber's thickness.

Soon Frank Junior takes his leave. The two are still talking as the younger man starts his car. The topic is Edd's last trip to California. Edd looks out over a green wilderness that stretches away far beyond his neat house. Visitors who come here to buy dulcimers tell him they would love to spend their summers at this spot. Edd speaks of the mountains:

"I always thought the Rocky Mountains was like those mountains you see here—covered with trees and all. But, by golly, they ain't nothing but rocks."

Frank Junior now drives off and passes the pond and the fields. He looks back at the long view of the northwest peaks that he can see close up at his Potter-town home. He drives up the hill on Old Mountain Road and continues past the turnoff to the Hicks graveyard. Although he never lived here, this is the cradle of his world. It is just as it was when his mother and Ray walked barefoot to their grandparents' home, less than a hundred yards from where Edd and Nettie now live.

At the blue mailbox up from Ray and Rosa's house, Frank Junior stops and draws his dulcimer and banjo from the rear seat. He walks down past the springhouse and the giant ash tree where more than a half-century ago his father, Frank Senior, joined Nathan, Roby, and other kinsmen to play for the ballad collectors from New York.

Ray Hicks greets his nephew heartily, seeming to become a young man again. Rosa has hot food ready, and Frank Junior joins them at the kitchen table. Ray laughs and tells stories, just as the visitor wants and expects. Rosa smiles quietly, enjoying the repartee that comes after the stories.

The Passing of the Torch

When they finish eating, Ray settles his long frame into the chair in front of the cold stove; he rolls a cigarette and grins so that the corners of his eyes crinkle elfishly.

"Yea, Franklin, play 'Shake Hands with Mother Again,'" he commands.

Frank Junior sits forward, still tuning the banjo, his head cocked as though to feel the vibrations. Then, his handsome banjo in tune, he sits back and begins to play. The room grows lighter as the strings are plucked. He sings:

If I could be there when Jesus comes
And know the day and hour.
I'd like to be standing at Mother's tomb
When Jesus comes in His power.

'Twill be a wonderful, happy day
Up there on the Golden Strand
When I can hear Jesus my Savior say,
"Shake hands with Mother again."

As Frank Junior begins the second verse, Ray joins in. He turns in his chair and keeps rhythm with his cigarette, bobbing it high and to the side:

I'd like to say, "Mother, this is your dear boy
That you left when you went away."
I'd like to say, "Mother, it gives me great joy
To see you again today."

'Twill be a wonderful, happy day
Up there on the Golden Strand,
When I can hear Jesus my Savior say,
"Shake hands with Mother again."

As the two pause at the end of the song, Ray's face beams in the same way it does when he finishes a Jack Tale. He says, "Franklin, you can make that thing talk, yiah. Now, you gonna try 'Tom Dooley'?"

Frank Junior nods and says he'll sing the same way his father sang it, sing the same lyrics the Kingston Trio picked up. Again he plays the banjo, and this time Ray does not join him. Enchanted, he listens.

When Frank Junior finishes, he talks about the ballad and how it was

The Passing of the Torch

among his father's first memories. When Frank Senior was no more than three years old, he had heard his own father, Wiley, sing it as he worked. The tune had been handed down in the family, but Frank Senior studied the history of the murder of Laura Foster, and it was he who added the lines about Dula's capture:

This time tomorrow,
Reckon where I'll be;
Hadn't been for Grayson
I'd be now in Tennessee.

[Colonel Grayson captured Tom Dula near Trade, on the Carolina-Tennessee border.]

Frank Junior now plays other songs for his uncle Ray, the liveliest being "Fly Around My Pretty Little Miss, Fly Around My Daisy":

Every time I go down the road,
Seems dark and cloudy.
Every time I see that gal,
She always hollers, "Howdy . . . "

Frank Junior puts down the banjo and takes up the dulcimer. He says a man over in Tennessee built the instrument, the one who apprenticed under Stanley Hicks. It has a dark, shiny body and obviously is not made in the primitive style Edd Presnell described as "the old way."

After the dulcimer is tuned, the visitor noodles varied tunes. Then he plays "Groundhog," "John Henry," "Wild Bill Jones." Finally, he begins to strum a tune that has survived from Old England.

"Hear these words," he says. "My dad told me the ballad goes back in the family beyond memory, and you'll know what he's talking about when you hear it. It's a song about a working man that one of the gentry in the Old Country wronged." Frank Junior plays and sings, and at times Ray joins him.

Bo Lamkin was as fine a mason
As ever laid a stone,
He built a fine castle
And pay he got none.

He swore to his God,
He'd kill them unknown;
Beware of Bo Lamkin
When I'm gone from home.

The ballad goes on to relate that when the lord was away, Bo Lamkin killed the lady of the castle and her baby. Frank Junior does not sing all the verses, but near the end the fate of Bo Lamkin is revealed:

Bo Lamkin was hung
To the scaffold so high . . .

Throughout the afternoon Frank Junior plays, with Ray sometimes singing along. At last, when he packs his instruments to go, all are smiling. The past has been revisited. The memory of Frank Senior, who died in 1965, is vivified for a brief time.

"He never cared about hillbilly singing," says Frank Junior. "He thought those professionals did not really care about how mountain people lived and where they came from."

Frank Senior worked as a carpenter and a logger. He rode the rails in the early thirties and took work where he could find it. For years he did not have a musical instrument of any kind, because he had sold them all to provide for his family. During the Great Depression he often sang "Hard Times on Beaverdam Road," a story he composed about his own mountain neighborhood; the song spread from Pickbritches throughout Appalachia and into other areas of the poor South.

On the eve of his sixty-eighth birthday, Ray Hicks sits on the wide, low porch of his house and sharpens his chain saw. He has been cutting wood for Rosa to burn in the kitchen stove. Rosa comes to the door and brings a chair for Ray's caller. She says she would like to stay and talk, but she has corn to can. It is a warm afternoon by mountain standards, and Ray's face is flushed and damp. He is cordial, but perhaps a visit with him today is an inconvenience.

"No, stay," he protests. "I'll be through here directly. Then we can talk a little."

Sitting on a dilapidated porch glider, Ray bends over the chain saw and carefully files its small blades. Although both he and Rosa are busy, they seem to work as with a hobby. Ray's hair is mussed and his eyes appear drawn; he says he hasn't been feeling well. "Kidneys, you know."

The soft, lazy humming of a summer day fills the air. Honey bees have some reason to dance and circle on the ceiling hex sign. A few flies crawl on the roughly hewn porch posts and on the windowsill of the room where Ray was "bairned" sixty-eight years before. Occasionally Ray stops his work, picks up a swatter, and holds it halfway up its wire handle, waiting for a fly to land. With a flip of the wrist, he brings the swatter head lightly and quickly down upon the insect. Smoke from Rosa's kitchen at times curls around the house, and the smell of burning oak brings up the subject of Ray's parlor stove, which had been a delight to his late cousin Stanley.

"Yiah, Stanley and everybody liked my invention," says Ray. "It's a stove my Dad bought, and if you don't care for its looks, it's still a good'un. I could have sold my invention if I could have made it pretty, shiny. But that wouldn't have matched people's houses, rough like it is. But it's a real invention for creosote."

The stove occupies the center of the sitting room and is tilted slightly toward its back, "which makes the fire hotter somehow." Its body is rectangular, and it has a flat top covered with a slab of bluish stone an inch thick, which Ray once hauled all the way from Cranberry.

"They's a lot of that stone over there. I didn't have to hew it any; just evened off the sides."

Atop the stone are layers of firewood, and from the back a pipe angles upward and bends across the room to a hole "that Dad pecked in the chimney when he decided it wasn't a fireplace he needed but a stove."

Attached to the stovepipe are tin cans filled with gravel and water and held in place by wires. The effect is whimsically complex, not unlike a Rube Goldberg cartoon.

"Soot and creosote would fill up the chimney and pipes," Ray says, "up till I studied it and figgered a remedy to stop it."

Ray says he does not know how the stone, the wood, the cans, and the gravel eliminate creosote, but the combination works.

"I used to have to get up there and freeze in the winter, cleaning out the chimney and all . . . every two or three weeks. See, the soot got in there and would hold the draft; and the creosote would catch on fire. Used to scare Mama to death.

"Now if you build a weak fire in it when it's warm, it'll soot up some, and when it gets cold and you get a pretty hot fire going, it'll burn gray and clean in there like a tailpipe on a good-tuned car." Again Ray explains that he was once an automobile mechanic, "mostly with my own tools."

A truck stops on the dusty road above the house. Three bearded men, large and brawny, come down the path by the springhouse. They talk softly and laugh. Ray does not appear to notice them. They stop, probably waiting to be invited onto the porch. Meanwhile they continue speaking in low tones and chuckling easily. Their ages seem to be between thirty-five and forty-five.

When Ray finishes telling of his days as a mechanic, the men shuffle onto the porch, dwarfing it. The tall one is Ted, Ray and Rosa's son who still lives at home. The stocky, black-bearded one is Orville Hicks, and the man with the flaxen beard is Benny Harmon, both Rosa's kinsmen. They are formidable in their overalls and adjustable caps; if they frowned rather than smiled, they would be the tough mountain men of adventure books.

But all appear good-humored, and they hunker down on the porch, still smiling.

"That's Orville there," says Ray, pointing to the stocky man. "He's been named a Kentucky Colonel, and him so young. Storytelling. Little kids love him. I teached him, and now he's better than me."

"No," protests Orville seriously. "I ain't the best." He points to Ray. "That there's the best. He's the king of them all." The others nod and banter as they laugh with Ray.

Ray says he wants Orville to tell a story. Orville demurs, but the other men cajole and prod him. Finally Orville begins to talk.

His stories are not Jack Tales. They are contemporary anecdotes and jokes; although he knows Ray's Jack Tales, he tells other stories, too—many that he has made up. Finishing one story, he says: "Now don't that remind you of 'Jack and the Three Sillies'?"

Now that Orville is talking, no more prompting is needed. He moves from story to story. His friends bend over laughing; they cut their eyes toward the guest to catch reactions. Orville is good-natured and humorous, and he enjoys his role. Ray is proud; he smiles widely and continually. Obviously, Orville is Ray's anointed torchbearer, even though the shy son, Ted, knows all Ray's stories. But Ted will succeed his father only as a hardworking heir in the potato

The Passing of the Torch

— 161 —

fields and in gathering herbs. His chosen mission seems to be taking care of his parents, not speaking before crowds.

The confabulation turns to changing times.

"Yiah, it was when power and lights came to the mountains that ways started being different," says Ray. "But most of the old people was gone by then anyway. Yiah, I knew all about the old days. I was in my thirties before they got co-op lines in here."

"And the roads that came in here, not much good, but they brought a few cars," says Benny.

"They ain't much better now," says Ray.

Orville agrees that the coming of electricity marked the point when mountain living began to move toward contemporary standards. He is not sure he is among the moderns: "I was thirteen before we had lights," he recalls. "Electricity came to the mountains somewhere about the time I was born. But we were so poor that it was the sixties before we could afford it. One time we got a bill for three dollars, and Dad said if it ever went that high again he'd cut it off. He let us use lights for a half-hour; then we had to go to bed."

Orville's father was a Baptist preacher, but he had no license to preach and no car. He and his wife walked to wherever a meeting was held, taking along their brood of seven boys and four girls.

"He was strict and he'd whop us if we didn't walk the straight and narrow," says Orville. "He caught me shooting marbles under the church and gave me a whipping."

Food, however, was not lacking; Orville's family ate well. Once, during a blizzard in which the snow drifted to seventeen feet, a helicopter dropped food onto the farm.

"But we didn't really need food," says Orville. "Had plenty in the cellar. But the chocolate bars were something we didn't get often.

"A neighbor somehow got word to the Red Cross that she needed a bale of hay for her cow. The helicopter came over, dropped the hay, and it fell on the cow. Killed it, it did."

When Orville isn't working or running with his friends Ted and Benny, he's telling stories. He goes to schools all over western North Carolina and to some churches.

"My daddy didn't approve my telling stories. He said he was out trying to tell the people the truth, and here I'm out telling lies."

The Passing of the Torch

But Orville thinks storytelling is his charge in life. His great-grandfather, Council Harmon, was a tale spinner of legend in these parts, and on Orville's calling cards there is the line: "In Memory of Council Harmon." He thinks storytelling is far from dead.

Ray asks Orville to tell the story about "The Good Man and the Bad Man." Orville laughs and begins:

There were two older fellows. One would give you the shirt off his back, the other was mean and greedy. One Sunday they walked together in the woods. Down an old path they saw a little bird on the ground, its wing broke. The good man picked up the bird. He said he'd take it home and care for it. The mean man said, "Throw that bird down and let's go on."

But the good man took the bird home, fed it, watered it, mended its wing. Then one day the little bird was ready to fly, but first it turned and gave the good man a seed. Told him that would be his fortune.

So the good man planted the seed in his garden. One morning he went out and saw cucumbers all over the ground. He cut into the largest and found gold and silver. Every one of the cucumbers was like that. "I'm rich, I'm rich," he said. He ran to tell the mean man.

"Why do good things happen to everybody but me?" cried the mean man.

Then the mean man told the good man he'd find his own little bird.

He went to the woods but couldn't find a bird. Then the next morning he took his slingshot, put a rock in it, and shot a bird, breaking its wing. He picked up the bird.

"Poor little bird," he said. "I'm going to take you home."

The mean man fed, watered, and took care of the bird, and when the bird was ready to fly, it turned and gave the man a seed. Told the mean man to plant it in his garden. It would be his fortune.

"Good," said the mean man. "I'm going to be rich like my neighbor."

He planted the seed, watered, and hoed it, but when the vines began to grow they grew straight up and had no cucumbers on them.

One day the mean man went out and found the vine had growed all the way to the moon. He said, "That's where my fortune's at . . . on the moon."

So he clumb and clumb and clumb until he got to the top of the vine and stepped off on the moon. He looked back at the vine, but it had withered already.

The Passing of the Torch

So, when you walk out tonight, look up to the moon. The dark spot you see is the mean man. He'll always be there.

The men on the porch laugh, and Ray says when he was a boy he had wanted to go to the moon: "See, back when we growed up in the mountains, my mama would tell us that the dark spot on the moon was there because a man burnt brush on Sunday, and God put him there to burn brush forever and ever.

"When I's little I'd look at the moon and want to climb up there and help the man."

Now the men seem to look to Ray to pick up the stories; they are accustomed to Ray's being the focus of any gathering. But after telling of his boyhood wish to help the man on the moon, Ray looks off toward the Rock of Lost Gold. He grins elfishly as though thinking of a funny thing to say.

Orville, sure he is no longer on center stage, lights a storebought cigarette and leans against a porch post. The men are silent as they wait for Ray to take over; they are ready to laugh and slap their thighs as they always do.

Then Ray turns toward the men. He says it is no wonder that Orville was named a Kentucky Colonel and that children love him.

"Orville's the one that'll carry on," says Ray. "He'll keep 'em laughing long atter I'm gone."

It is an uncomfortable moment. Ray seems wistfully to proffer the torch to his black-bearded kinsman. He looks gratefully toward Orville and remembers that "not many are left to learn the world how the old people lived."

Ray will go back to the storytelling festival in Tennessee in October, and he likes it that so many people tell new stories they've made up, but he says ways of living are changing, that the old stories are dying out and people do not sing the old songs as much as they did when he was growing up.

"I guess that's why I was put here—to sing the songs, to tell the stories, to let the people know how they can live off the bare earth if it ever comes to that again."

He says that David Hicks, Stanley's only son, does not carry on the tradition. David once told him that he'd like to play as his father did, "but I can't even play a radio without it staticking up on me."

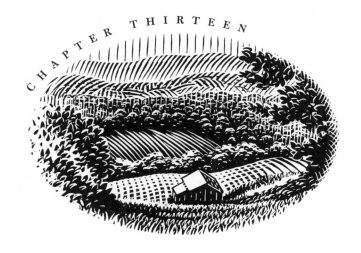

CHAPTER THIRTEEN

Looking Back from Devil's Claw

It is late summer, and the new day's sun emerges bright and metallic, a silver dollar gleaming through the settled mist below. More than two hundred years ago—even before the first Hickses inhabited these mountains—Bishop August Spangenberg looked down from a then-unnamed peak into the valleys of Watauga. Seeking a place to establish a Moravian colony, he wrote of "hundreds of mountain peaks all about us, presenting a spectacle like ocean waves in a storm."

This morning, to the east, those same valleys are enshrouded in great billows that are pierced by the mountain peaks—cobalt islands in a white sea. To the south are two dark sentinels. One the settlers called "Dunvegan"; the greater one, across the Watauga Valley, they named "Grandfather," because at least two rocky profiles resemble an old man. Grandfather is said to be the world's oldest mountain, and tomorrow Fran and I are to take Ray and Rosa Hicks there to visit a menagerie near its top.

Several times André Michaux, botanist to France's Louis XVI, came to these peaks to collect plants. In 1794, Michaux climbed the stony sides of Grandfather Mountain to reach a promontory now known as Calloway Peak, a summit that rises so high from its base that the Frenchman thought he had discovered North America's tallest mountain. He wrote in his journal that on August 30 he stood atop the pinnacle with his companion and guide and sang his country's anthem, "La Marseillaise." Thus he paid tribute to his native France but exulted in America's majesty.

Indeed, Grandfather is the monarch of the Blue Ridge, but several other mountain systems join the Blue Ridge to make up the Appalachian chain. Within these are many peaks that soar higher than Grandfather, but none are so esteemed for their beauty and stateliness.

This morning it is cool and quiet as I walk northerly on the saddle of Four Diamond Ridge—so close to Grandfather that I can make out individual trees silhouetted on the great mountain's crest. At the road's end is a Gibraltar-like rock that shades the northern side and is pocked with dark caves. There is little doubt that this granite rose upon the earth in the same cataclysmic instant as did Grandfather Mountain. The rock's lichen-covered ledges tell how rhododendron and dwarf trees gained a toehold, how the drab green algae and microfungi trapped humus particles to make a food base for inchoative plant growth. They formed an underlayer upon which wind and flying creatures deposited seeds. On the sheer sides there are plants that seem to grow directly out of the stone. The monolith harbors ancient secrets, its dark mass eclipsing the brilliance of the morning.

Beyond the road's end, I pick my way through thorn trees and low brambles. My plan is to climb Hanging Rock, the same mile-high peak that Ray Hicks could see on his way to school sixty years before. Its craggy top is easily visible from Mt. Mitchell more than fifty miles to the south, from Tennessee's Roan Mountain to the west, from Mt. Jefferson far to the north, and from Blowing Rock to the nearby east. When young Margaret Shomaker played upon the knoll behind her family's house, before the tragic landslide of 1940, she rested against its boulders and dreamed of standing atop the distant Hanging Rock. The distinctive profile had long proved a trusty guidon for settlers on their journeys.

We know from journals that Michaux recognized Hanging Rock's botanical importance, and that in 1841 Asa Gray found on its north face a rare plant he named "spreading avens." Today avens and other rare species, including the wretched sedge, grow here under the protection of conservationists. I do not plan to invade that side of the mountain. Instead, I expect to climb the eastern slope and reach the mile-high apex; from there I will look out to see Bishop Spangenberg's "spectacle like ocean waves in a storm." Also, through binoculars I want to look around the eastern slopes of Beech Mountain, to search out faraway Devil's Highway and the scene of the "bustout." I have, long before, ventured over those primitive roads, those forests, those valleys of the Hicks environs; today I will look down upon them as though they were part of a raised topographical map.

Soon the soil underfoot gives way to slabs of granite, and the terrain bends sharply upward. Over steep boulders I pick my way, sure that Hanging Rock's peak is only yards away. At the top, I find the granite weathered to a razor's edge; it is not the level summit I expected. Grasping the rim, I swivel to look across the ravine. I have lost my way. Instead of reaching Hanging Rock, I have become disoriented by the brambles and have scaled the eerie convexity known by pioneers as Devil's Claw.

I hold to the edge, staying until my limbs are spent. This has been an unfriendly climb, and I do not intend to make it again. Still, now that I am here, I will enjoy a view similar to that from the taller Hanging Rock. I will admire what Ray Hicks calls "God's creation."

From Devil's Claw, it is easy to see that the highlands are corroding. As recently as when Ray Hicks courted Rosa Harmon at Sandy Flat—a locale I can see clearly from my perch—the roads were narrow and did not leave stark gashes in the earth. No second homes scarred the ridges; vacationing invaders were scarce. Streams ran sparkling and free of silt, and the sky was clear of contrails.

Around the curve of Beech Mountain's north slope, in the vicinity of Ray and Rosa's home, there still exist vestiges of early American life—dulcimer makers, cabbage farmers, storytellers, ballad singers, hunters, and herb gatherers. One by one they turn down their lanterns, but those who remain are treasures; they form a bridge between contemporary America and the Europe of more than two centuries ago. The fact that a few still live reminds us that even in its despoliation, the earth is still young.

Tomorrow Fran and I will travel twisting, stony roads into the secretive land of the Hickses; we plan to take them to Grandfather Mountain and then to our home for dinner.

"Yiah," Ray said. "I've heared about where you live there near the Hanging

Rock; heared the wind blows hard and it's awful cold in winter. I've not been there but I want to see where you live."

With Ray and Rosa as passengers, we will stop at a place along Devil's Highway, and I will point out the profile of the distant Devil's Claw, nestled below Hanging Rock, a jutting landmark they have known all their lives. Then I will trace the mountain's rim southward to where we live, just over the edge to one of the legions of encroachments upon the wild lands where still today foxes, squirrels, rabbits, opossums, and groundhogs make their homes. Even a few wildcats live in the caves near Devil's Claw.

The sun climbs directly overhead, and the blue of the sky fades as I make my way off the ridge, arms and legs weary but eyes never tiring of the grandeur. When Ray calls it "God's creation," he does not care that geologists have long debated and revised their assessments of the region's genesis. To his way of thinking, the peaks and valleys were put here by a higher being. There are no cosmic questions to answer, no mysteries to solve.

Back through the brambles and scattered boulders I meander home. Fog has now obscured the azure sky, and I tread through it along the mountain road. Clouds blow in the wind, and it is strange that the wisps never seem to reach me; they pass well away on either side, seeming always to be somewhere else.

In the fading afternoon, the curtain of fog draws aside, and the stage becomes an expanse of damp summer colors against a washed sky. I sit in the swing and lazily scan the valley. Fran comes to the door and tells me she thinks she will not go to Grandfather Mountain, that she wants to spend the time preparing for Ray and Rosa's visit.

Then, as evening approaches, a wren that has reared two broods near the deck alights on its house; it begins singing and its songs are as melodious as a mockingbird's. A monarch butterfly twitches and wafts in the cool air, and wildflowers toss on the high meadow. As the sun drops beyond Beech and Big Pine Mountains, the shadows of Hanging Rock and Devil's Claw stretch over the valley. At last an owl calls from somewhere beyond the ridge.

At ten minutes to three the following day, I stop on the road above Ray and Rosa's home and see an out-of-state vehicle parked by the mailbox. Since I am early, I will knock at the open door and tell the Hickses I will be ready when they are. Stepping onto the porch, I see a visitor inside hurrying between microphones and sound machinery. He greets me cheerfully, but Ray seems preoccupied. Thinking that perhaps we will be late getting away, I go down to the backside garden and walk among Rosa's flowers. Presently there comes a call: "Robert. You ready to go?"

It is Ray, and I hurry to the front of the house, where he and Rosa are brightly dressed and smiling.

"You sure you're finished?" I ask, seeing the visitor at the door, his equipment still in place.

"Yiah," Ray answers. "Me'n Rosa's ready to go."

"But your visitor . . . "

"Aw, he don't mind; he knows we was expecting you."

The man waves wanly. If he had counted on Ray and Rosa to delay their outing, he might have been disappointed. In the car I ask Ray if the man had gotten all he needed.

"I hope so," says Ray. "He's a nice feller and I told him Jack Tales. But he knew you was a-coming."

Ray sits on the passenger side up front, his long legs drawn up against the glove compartment. He rolls a cigarette, and Rosa tells him that maybe I do not want him to smoke in the car. True, there have never been ashes in the tray, but Ray tells Rosa I won't mind. The car groans up the unpaved road and past a small house set back among the weeds, its tin roof rusting.

Ray points with his cigarette: "Now that's where me'n Rosa lived when we's first married, until Jack got drowned and we had to move down and live with Mama. And on up yander, high up the mountain over them trees, is where the men hid their gold—remember?—and thought they'd killed the Indian guide."

We climb higher on the eastern side of Beech Mountain and drive past homes of Ray's relatives. The enormous valley below spreads to a majestic line of mountains, the same peaks that Rosa sees when she pulls back the curtains of her kitchen each morning. We pass a large home on a knoll, and Ray points again:

"That's where my cousin lives, and right down here is where I had my wreck."

On a Christmas Eve one year, after Ray and Rosa's children were grown, Ray came home in a blizzard. His headlights had been wrongly adjusted at an in-

Looking Back from Devil's Claw

spection station, he said, and the beams shot upward so that it was difficult to see the road in the drifting snow. As he reached the crest of the hill, his pickup slipped off the road and tumbled end over end down a deep ravine.

"Just dropped off," Ray says, shaking his head, "like it fell out of a tree."

Ray lay half-conscious at the foot of the slope until at last he managed to crawl uphill a hundred yards to his cousin's house. Days later it was discovered that among his many injuries was a broken neck.

"And down yander, see that white house? That's where Andrew Jackson and Suzy Ann lived, my grandparents. And that little building is the store they ran."

It was there that Ray bought candy for young Rosa and her family, and there that Grandmother Suzy Ann once told him, "If you can get Dory's girl, you'd better be a-jumping."

Soon Rosa is pointing to the southeast:

"You wanted to see where I was born. Look way over there. There's a light a-shining right on the spot." Something metal, perhaps even the tin roof of the Harmons' old house, reflects the brilliance of the afternoon sun.

A pickup truck approaches, billowing dust behind. The driver crowds us to the side and salutes merrily as he passes.

"Know him?" I ask.

"Naw," Ray shakes his head. "People always wave."

Farther down the road a dark-haired girl comes along more slowly in a small car. She steers well to her right and waves. We all wave back.

After turning off the long Andy Hicks Road, we drive past a large, listing barn that was once a cheese factory; it was one of the few enterprises in the area when Ray was a boy. After this there is a fork in the road and a brick church close by.

"This used to be a wood church, were we went," says Rosa.

It is the place where the Voice said to Ray, "That's your wife."

The creek we pass was the spot Ray where jumped on the pickup and lodged his foot between the bumper and the truck bed.

The open view to the valley of the far mountains is now blocked by trees as the road veers farther to the upside of the hill. Soon we pass a dense wooded patch where one tree, near the road, grows out of the ground at a slanting angle and then rises straight up. On this tree, Nathan Hicks hanged himself forty-five years earlier. It is a painful memory, and Ray does not look.

Ray and Rosa become more animated as we drive across the land on which much of their past unfolds.

"Now there," Ray points. "See that big barn? It sits right where I went to school. And up here on the knoll is where the bustout came and washed away the Shomaker house."

At the menagerie on Grandfather Mountain, Ray looks intently at a pair of bald eagles perched on a fallen limb. Above the humming chatter of tourists, a man —apparently the father of three boys who wear prep school shirts and run about noisily—speaks pedantically and loudly. Ray does not seem to notice but turns to a knot of visitors and talks easily to them, as though they are old friends:

"Now my granddaddy, John Benjamin Hicks," Ray begins, "when he was a baby, a bald-headed eagle like that swooped down and was a-going to carry him away. . . ." The listeners smile and are attentive as this tall mountain man—his voice and phrasing new and foreign to them—continues to talk. The loud man turns quiet and looks sourly toward Ray. As he herds the boys along, one turns and asks, "Who *was* that?" The man shakes his head slowly; Ray does not notice.

There are bears to visit, but Rosa has been told that panthers, or mountain lions, are housed nearby, and she wants to see them now. At the open barrier, she cannot locate the animals; they are hidden behind huge boulders scattered about the grounds below. Minutes pass and we wait to leave, but Rosa is intent upon seeing the animals.

During Rosa's childhood in Sandy Flat, she heard mountain lions shriek from the top of Rocky Face, and she remembered the oft-told story of her aunt carrying a small child on a moonlit night. As the aunt entered the yard of her home, a giant cat leaped screaming from the shadows into her path. The woman's eyes darted frantically about, and she saw there was no escape. If she ran toward the road, the panther would overtake her, and already it blocked the entrance to her house. Whether from bravery or fright—she never knew—she suddenly screamed back, and the beast whirled and fled along the top of a chestnut fence.

Ray had often told Rosa of encounters with mountain lions in the forests at night—of how one man heard dripping noises, and when he beamed his lantern toward a tree limb he saw that the trickling came from the blood of his dog, which the mountain lion now feasted upon.

The memories of great cats screaming from Rocky Face in the night have always fascinated Rosa. Now, at the menagerie, a panther saunters from behind its rock shelter to drink. Rosa stares for a long while; finally she turns to leave.

Mountain lions supposedly vanished from the Appalachian wild forty years ago, and Rosa was a young bride when the last one was seen on Rocky Face. "Always wanted to see one up close," she says. "Another thing I'd like to see is the ocean."

In the nature museum, Ray towers over all the other visitors. He wears a leisure coat, overalls, and an army fatigue hat. In the lights of the museum his blue eyes glitter. As he studies plant and rock exhibits, milling visitors look upon this tall and mysterious man; they steal glances as he talks with Rosa.

A clean-cut young man approaches.

"Are you Mister Hicks?"

Ray nods.

"Mister Hicks, I grew up off Dark Ridge. I've heard of you since I was a child."

Ray grins. He tells the stranger how he used to see mountain lions in the forests of Dark Ridge.

At dinner I ask Ray to tell Fran how he won Rosa, and how the Voice spoke to him and told him she would be his wife. Because at the time I have not fully pieced together the sequences of their courtship, I seek answers from Rosa also. The two talk excitedly, often laughing, sometimes disagreeing. Since they do not frequently call up those younger days, there are occasional gaps and vague memories. But before the evening's end they hammer out the events and times of decades ago.

For the Hickses, the day has been long, and they ask to be taken back to Old Mountain Road—only a few miles but forty minutes distant.

It is a moonless night, and except for the headlights there is no illumination after we turn off the old Valle Crucis highway and start a twenty-five-minute drive over dirt roads. At last we turn down Old Mountain Road and see a faint light through the trees above the Hicks home. We stop by the blue mailbox, and Fran stays in the car as the Hickses and I follow my flashlight's beam down the grassy slope and past the ash tree and the springhouse. Ray and Rosa chat excitedly; they say they have enjoyed the outing, but they seem happy to be home. Through the windows of this, the oldest dwelling on Beech Mountain, we can see by the glimmer of a small lamp the dark forms of Ted, Benny, and Orville. They are playing poker with worn cards; their stakes are kitchen matches.

The automobile's lights again pierce sheer darkness as Fran and I travel homeward over Beech Mountain's eastern slopes; the scene passes like images in a three-dimensional film. Rural mailboxes loom and fade like Burma-Shave signs; they identify those who live in these now-darkened wayside homes. Their names are Ward, Presnell, Yates, Michael, Rominger. Their forebears figure prominently in the rhetoric and recall of the Hickses.

To the right, the earth sweeps up to the mountain's pinnacle, more than a thousand feet higher and less than three miles distant. Yet except for the road shoulders illuminated by our headlamps, there is nothing to see except shadowy forms of hillocks and a few farm buildings. To the left, the terrain drops off toward the Laurel Creek Valley, and tiny lights spread for miles—twinkling jewels on a great cloak of black velvet. As late as the Christmas Eve when Ray's pickup tumbled over the edge of the road, this necklace of lights did not glow in the valley, but even with its growth, Ray and Rosa attest that through the window of a morning the scene—the granite profiles of Hanging Rock, Rocky Face, Tester, Baird, and Valle Mountains—looks much the same as when they were young.

As always, the summer night is cool, but I open the windows to flush out a lingering odor of Ray's Prince Albert tobacco. The rush of air suddenly brings magic. Now we hear the wild sounds of summer—the startling flap of wings of a night bird flushed from the roadside, the insistent barking of a young fox, the rush of water as we cross the creek where the young Rosa admonished Ray long ago: "Get that big old hand off me."

But the ancient world of the Hickses begins to fall away as we turn onto Devil's Highway. Soon the landscape becomes pitted with lights from picture windows. Homes of newcomers from the lowlands dot the ridges where Bynum Shomaker harvested cabbages and where Ed Chappell's land rises over its nearly four hundred acres to a lofty knoll. The site is so awesomely beautiful that Ed would not clutter it by raising a home there.

Beyond the blueberry farm, at the end of Lee Gwaltney road, we emerge entirely from the enchanted land of the Hickses. We turn right and drive west along Shawneehaw Creek, the very road on which Naomi Shomaker and her daughter Margaret, victims of the "Forty Flood" bustout, were taken to the hospital. At the hardware store the road dips to its lowest level; here Ed Chappell jumped into the water fully clothed and risked his own life to help lift Naomi's and Margaret's heads above the floodwaters.

We are entering Banner Elk, now a growing commercial center with its expanding student population and nearby golf and ski enterprises. A family named Banner once owned these acres on the north bank of the Elk River, and locals distinguished it from the land on the south bank by calling it *Banner's* Elk—the way Ray Hicks and the old-timers still refer to it.

At the town's only stoplight, the enchantment of the Hicks country at last yields to reality. It is now that Fran breaks a reverie of many miles:

"They are so gracious," she declares. "I believe Rosa and Ray envy no one on earth."

SOURCES

Arthur, John Preston. *Western North Carolina: A History, 1730–1913*. Chapel Hill: University of North Carolina Press, 1914.

Blackmun, Ora. *Western North Carolina: Its Mountains and Its People to 1880*. Boone, N.C.: Appalachian Consortium Press, 1977.

Dugger, Shepherd M. *The Balsam Groves of Grandfather Mountain*. Philadelphia: J. B. Lippincott Company, 1892.

Hicks, John Henry, Mattie Hicks, and Barnabas B. Hicks. *The Hicks Families of Western North Carolina*. Boone, N.C.: Minor's Printing, 1991.

Kephart, Horace. *Our Southern Highlanders*. New York: Macmillan Publishing Company, 1913.

Robinson, Blackwell P., ed. *The North Carolina Guide*. Chapel Hill: University of North Carolina Press, 1955.

Van Noppen, Ina W., and John J. Van Noppen. *Western North Carolina since the Civil War*. Boone, N.C.: Appalachian Consortium Press, 1973.

Warner, Anne. *Traditional American Folk Songs*. Syracuse, N.Y.: Syracuse University Press, 1984.

THE HICKS LINE
(*Abridged*)

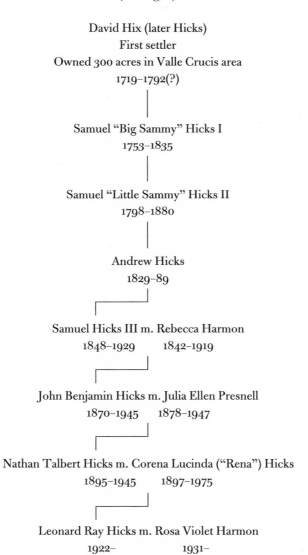

David Hix (later Hicks)
First settler
Owned 300 acres in Valle Crucis area
1719–1792(?)

Samuel "Big Sammy" Hicks I
1753–1835

Samuel "Little Sammy" Hicks II
1798–1880

Andrew Hicks
1829–89

Samuel Hicks III m. Rebecca Harmon
1848–1929   1842–1919

John Benjamin Hicks m. Julia Ellen Presnell
1870–1945   1878–1947

Nathan Talbert Hicks m. Corena Lucinda ("Rena") Hicks
1895–1945   1897–1975

Leonard Ray Hicks m. Rosa Violet Harmon
1922–   1931–

Rena Hicks, wife of Nathan and mother of Ray, was a daughter of Andrew Jackson Hicks (1877–1949) and Susan Ann Presnell Hicks (1881–1951). Andrew Jackson Hicks was a son of Samuel Hicks III and Rebecca Harmon; he was a brother of John Benjamin Hicks.

Stanley Hicks (1911–1989), "double first cousin" of Ray, was a son of Roby Hicks (1882–1957) and Buena Vista ("Buny") Presnell Hicks (1888–1984). His father's parents were Samuel and Rebecca, and his brothers included John Benjamin Hicks, Ray's grandfather. Stanley married Virgie Pressley; their only son, David Hicks, is still living.

Rosa Hicks, wife of Ray, was a daughter of Lee Monroe Harmon (1890–1973) and Mary Ellen McGuire (??–1971). Her grandfather, McKeller ("Kell") Harmon (1863–1950), was married to Susan Presnell (1884–1946). The Harmon line in America began with George Hermann (1710–1787), a German-Austrian immigrant.

John Henry Hicks, Mattie Hicks, and Barnabas B. Hicks, writing in their 1991 book *The Hicks Families of Western North Carolina* (from which most of this genealogy is derived), declare that Council Harmon, born on the Watauga River, is an "oft-cited" source of English folktales handed down by the Hicks family.